1995

NEW

selected poems 1950–2000

D0761256

WESLEYAN POETRY

ALSO BY NATHANIEL TARN:

Old Savage/Young City (1964)
Thirteen to Bled (1965)
Selection: Penguin Modern Poets, 7 (1965)
Where Babylon Ends (1967)
The Beautiful Contradictions (1969)
October (1969)
The Silence (1969)
A Nowhere for Vallejo (1971)
Section: The Artemision (1973)
Le Belle Contradizzione (tr. R. Sanesi, 1973)
The Persephones (1974)
Lyrics for the Bride of God (1975)
Narrative of this Fall (1975)
The House of Leaves (1976)
The Microcosm (1977)
The Ground of Our Great Admiration of Nature (w. Janet Rodney, 1977)
The Forest (w. Janet Rodney, 1978)
Birdscapes, with Seaside (1978)
Atitlán/Alashka (*Alashka* w. Janet Rodney) (1979)
The Land Songs (1981)
Weekends in Mexico (1982)
The Desert Mothers (1984)
At the Western Gates (1985)
Palenque (1986)
The Mothers of Matagalpa (1989)
Seeing America First (1989)
Home One (1990)
The Army Has Announced That Body Bags . . . (1992)
Caja del Río (1992)
Flying the Body (1993)
A Multitude of One (by Natasha Tarn, ed. by Nathaniel Tarn), (1994)
The Architextures 1–7 (1999)
The Architextures (2000)

Poems 1985–1998
Three Letters from the City: The St. Petersburg Poems (2001)

TRANSLATIONS:

The Heights of Macchu Picchu (Neruda) (1966)
Con Cuba (1969)
Stelae (Segalen) (1969)
Selected Poems (Neruda) (1970)
The Rabinal Achi, Act 4 (1973)
The Penguin Neruda (1975)

PROSE:

Views from the Weaving Mountain: Selected Essays in Poetics & Anthropology (1991)
Scandals in the House of Birds: Shamans & Priests on Lake Atitlán (1998)

Selected Poems

1950–2000

Nathaniel Tarn

Wesleyan University Press

MIDDLETOWN, CONNECTICUT

Published by Wesleyan University Press, Middletown, CT 06459
This collection © 2002 by Nathaniel Tarn
All rights reserved
Printed in the United States of America
5 4 3 2 1

CIP data apear at the back of the book

ACKNOWLEDGMENTS FOR PREVIOUSLY PUBLISHED MATERIAL
PUBLISHED IN BOOK FORM:

Old Savage/Young City. London: Jonathan Cape, 1964; New York: Random House, 1965.
Where Babylon Ends. New York: Richard Grossman, 1967; London: Cape Goliard Press, 1968.
October. London: Trigram Press, 1969.
The Beautiful Contradictions. London: Cape Goliard Press, 1969; New York: Random House, 1970.
A Nowhere for Vallejo. New York: Random House, 1971; London: Jonathan Cape, 1972.
The Persephones. Santa Barbara, CA: Christopher's Books, 1974.
Lyrics for the Bride of God. New York: New Directions, 1975; London: Jonathan Cape, 1976.
The House of Leaves. Santa Barbara, CA: Black Sparrow Press, 1976.
The Microcosm. Milwaukee, WI: Membrane Press, 1977.
Birdscapes, with Seaside. Santa Barbara, CA: Black Sparrow Press, 1976.
Atitlán/Alashka. Boulder, CO: Brillig Works, 1979.
The Desert Mothers. Granada, MS. Salt-Works Press, 1984.
At the Western Gates. Santa Fe, NM: Tooth of Time Press, 1985.
Seeing America First. Minneapolis, MN: Coffee House Press, 1989.
The Mothers of Matagalpa. London: Oasis Press, 1989.
Flying the Body. Los Angeles, CA: Arundel Press, 1993.
The Architextures. Tucson, AZ: Chax Press, 2000.
Three Letters from the City: The St. Petersburg Poems, 1968–98. Santa Fe: Weaselsleeves Press &
    St. Petersburg: Borey Arts Center, 2001.

NOT PUBLISHED IN BOOK FORM:

"Breughel at Wien." *Notus,* 10 (1992): 61–63.
"Segalen (Victor) Travels with Gauguin (Paul) . . ." *To,* 3–4 (1994): 8–13.
"Miniatures, Rajasthan/Punjab Hills." *That,* 20 (1994): no pagination.
"Bartók in Udaipur." *Conjunctions,* 17 (1991): 167–170.
"Aspens this Fall." *Grand Street,* 46 (1993): 46–48.
"Petals and Hair." *First Intensity,* 2 (1994): 24–25.
"Meditation: First and Last Trek, Zangskar." *Conjunctions,* 22 (1994): 184–189.
"Between a Death and Death." *Poetry New York,* 6 (1993–4): 48.
"Siempre Mas Invisible (Two)." *First Intensity,* 5 (1995): 39–40; *Oasis,* 75 (1995): 2–3; *The Capilano
    Review,* II, 17–18 (1996): 182–183.
"Red Banner's Whereabouts." *Conjunctions,* 20 (1993): 140–143; *First Offense,* 8 (1993): 45–49.
"An Interval." *First Intensity,* 10, (1998): 6–10.
"The Wisdom Roses." *Hambone,* 14 (1998): 28–29

31143007567523
811.54 Tarn
Tarn, Nathaniel.
Selected poems :
1950-2000

For the future:
Benjamin, Katya, Joshua, and . . .

contents

old savage/young city

For P.R.T.

OLD SAVAGE/YOUNG CITY

I

From the inner skin of my dreams,
from the womb's lining turned inside out,
where the soaring pine once nestled;
from the capsized backbone of my iron ship
that ploughed the rorqual, now a harpoon
thrust navel-deep into the fallow sky,
this knowledgeable heart, magic artificer,
convenes the mystery of all that I have ever known
and I find myself delighted again to belong to this world.

Streets like flexed muscles cannot knock me out:
I guess as far as power reaches, or indifference,
and then I have grown so used to sleepwalking
that sleep's no problem now.

Early I acquired the habit of looking for the eternal side of things,
tried to accomplish, in silence, what enthusiasts by the score
never even wished to begin. All for a smile's sake,
chivalrous above each proffered sacrifice.
Thus I cannot be frightened by these heroic tantrums,
this evangelism in the canyons of noon.
With trust in the continuity of all action
and stillness where the crowd core pulses;
frequently knowing I end a deed in its beginning,
tender in nurturing my small mistakes
in the daily quest for equilibrium between love and solitude,
I condemn them, knowing that I am ever of this life.
Delighted to belong to this world in my own autumn,
because I never take without giving in return,
never allowing a present even a flutter in my hand,
yet only reciprocating at the long long last
when the donor has forgotten what he gave—

for everything surrounding me forgets,
cities lose remembrance in their veins,
their ceremonial pattern fades,
their quick-step echoes die away,

only the shaman frolics, mocking his own mask,
whole capitals crumbling while he counts his fingers . . .

an honest servant accused of selfishness!

II

That which achieves its little ends by little means consoles me:
in a mausoleum details matter:

The way in which a nail mates with its wall,
a doormat yields under the feet of those who go in and out,
a door knob cools a sweating hand,

put me in touch with lives I have had difficulty in reconciling,
open the algebraic eyes of paradise.

III

There is not enough room in the sausage factories
so they take new measures and kill pigs in the street.
We do that, now and again, inside our community houses
but only when some important day of the gods is at hand.

Here there is no sign of the gods in the streets
and everyone walks by without raising his hat.

Some pale eyes blink but forget soon enough.

IV

The solitary man responds to matter
by taking it with him,
anchored to his soles and heels.
Others wallow in their freehold muck,
deprived of the whitewashing dividend of visions.

He who laughs within himself as he gazes around him,
seeing nothing but his eyes' laughter in others' eyes,
bears his own problems on his own shoulders
like a diminutive circus of birds,
without ever traveling from one city to another,
ever crossing a street,
or leaving a room to go down into the street,
(and so forth)
whiling his dusks away going home,
recalling his own sky and humming a love song.

V

A body on the morning after love is a jungle of smells,
inexplorable as a swamp, its sex closed.
A city after two or three weeks of being lived in,
accumulating its more and more exasperated skyscrapers,
becomes a terrified hermaphrodite looking for itself.
Male endures, female forgets.

VI

Darker than my loves themselves darker than white:

Some capitol unscaled by technicians has engendered them
and dropped them on the streets
where they change in a trice to black swans.
Then positive is negative again within the camera,
the roofs close in with the grace of trees, excluding light.

Chocolate-eyed Cassandras, marvelous with hunger,
the black girls glisten as they walk away
more naked than if they were naked.

VII

The professional suburbs are peaceful.
Mr Western goes home, forgets time and space,
puts on a docile dressing-gown,
recovers his absolute self,
wires roses to his love.

Unless she calls from far away to say that, tonight,
she flatters another man, the next night weds another
and so until this time next week or the week after.

This anthropologist translates romance to ritual.
Each footnote's rare, already obsolete.

VIII

Eons of frustrated flight,
the queen's nuptial indifference,
profit us nothing.
By betting all on building, man alone destroys.

No eschatology distracts the ravaging bee
from voyage to the sun. But man eliminates
time's architecture in the plan,
each nail, each brick, each girder in the mould.

I remain, planted everywhere, like pine needles.
I slouch, unwieldy as a fossil beast.
I am the lodestar of all faces, the slumbering animal.

IX

A raven death hovers above the river
gray with sarcophagi.

If the other world, as some myths have it, were similar to ours
and if all the ocean liners went there together on a given day
sailing toward an identical fresh city
with legions of garish dead aboard
who would be helpless without their desks
and phones and sexy secretaries
or (talk of pleasures) without cigarettes
bitter and human by comparison with their smokers, still

somewhere before the latter end there should be pity for them:
the air might be yielding and tender a few feet above the water,
softer than in the whaling seas where coffins are of coral and amber.

X

My face, when all is said and done, looks like a city too,
each wrinkle a street more or less in shadows by the watch,
shallow or deep, depending on its traffic of emotions.

Sometimes I lift my arms to the sky like skyscrapers
to join in similar lament, with ships coming and going,
and sometimes my thoughts follow surprising highways
with very few crossroads and intersections.
Then my logic tightens and shines, especially at night,
for a wind-thrashed old lady walks beside me.

She is as beautiful as love.

On the day the earth achieved enlightenment—
as it is said: each blade of grass shall know itself
knowing the wind it bends to its own purpose—
on the day our people went down to the sea
and welcomed in the dead from the breakers,
feasting them for a week with nothing withheld,

before they took them back again to the shore;
on the day the living and the dead walked hand in hand,
harvesting to themselves their far-flung fathers
who had heaved with the whale in the deep
and haunted with their wings the arctic hare,
on that day I was exiled and came to this city.

She is as beautiful as love.

Can I ever forget her? Tonight, sitting here, now, together,
we could be anywhere in the world, in any season, at any moment—
I have gathered her to my arms as the pines gather birds,
I call her mother and all her age-mates mother, as I once did,
I call her sister, daughter, lover, wife, and all, as I once adored her,
by the same token of oblivion.

I am profoundly lonely within myself, lonely in the land's bowels,
as lonely as a man can be . . . but this is not her business.

Cities devour her face.

New York, 1953—Cambridge, 1963

where babylon ends

THE LAUREL TREE

Streamed in her thirty-third year as i surmise this girl of rivers
uncertain whether back or forward to flow the present difficult
poured where two seas fight shy of mingling
thrust through the midst of them and parted them and rose
clothed in no clothes and without ornament
onto the beach of this lemon country

       turtle as ageless as her sorrow stones
       lays amber from her eyes as her eggs fall
       turns to inhale the sea so she believes
       but follows death inland
       melts in her carapace

ironed to wafers by the sky
this is the sand-pan greased with oil
the only dent in mile on mile of beach
into which she fitted the shape of her beautiful years
we outsweated the sun on that day and nearly drowned each other
doing nothing beyond that to spice love

       tarantula lies with a stake through her loins
       her legs curl like the planets round the sun
       she slowly sails the day as if at ease
       her eggs meanwhile as bloodshot as the salmon's
       although unnatural

she washed the foam from her hair in the whipping waters
fulfilled her needs invisibly in the sea
stood up in a surf of salt-bleached dolls
came over to brood me where i lay in the thyme
the bees in her breasts wove the thrashing gorse
her down her mandorla of light

a messenger yes/no a semaphore
her black/white keys her in/out whirl of morse
hoopoe signals salvation deviously
closed are the doors of death by thy donations
in the bowl of her wings she awaits our alms

since when i have looked for her as far as the earth is pleased to turn
to make the ships glide by as if they did not move
with wings at their funnels and resounding names
since when i have brushed every inch of the earth with sunlight
to etch her out of her landscape who had fled from me
turning to fiber behind her navel my hot seed

suffering servants now
are black and smell and do not smile
they do not remain human very long when looked at
their childrens' chins are smelted to their chests
even a mother is at pains to love

she is turning to wood in my arms at the knot in her knees
the branches in her thighs the boughs from breasts to armpits
she is turning to wood in the hot furrow of her belly
where it curves to meet the crease under her spine
she is turning to wood between her lips she cannot talk
she is turning to wood along her fingers they will bear leaves

children unborn dream of lemons
flies suck the furrows in their faces
parched skin cracks
on certain sections the skin turns inside out
garbage in newspapers

as for the gathering in of her desires as for her age
should no one even look at us in the streets anymore as we pass
it is a long time none the less since we have been alone in joy
or since there has been a possibility of anything in our lives but joy
and yet though grateful for each other's coincidence at this time
we are happiness-blind

a year has died since that blue sky
since the wound in her fur hung with pearls
a sparrow nestles in the crook of a branch
we do not see the burning flesh behind it
it is essence of bird essence of love

grow to wood   lose your silks   develop habits   but do not leave
this servant who would lie and drift by you his worthless life
i call her gaze to prolong the branches
shape to the wind if there be any wind where we have been
wake o my suffering hands upon your suffering hands
let them fall with the leper's thumb into the bowl out of our means

PROJECTIONS FOR AN EAGLE ESCAPED IN THIS CITY, MARCH 1965

AND HOW I BARE YOU ON EAGLES' WINGS

Toward the poem
as toward
any winter initiative,
fatigue cubes effort.
To be evil is nothing but to be tired,
selling short takes little more than to be weary,
those born to stumble claim no redress.
                wrong done to them
                is wrong in general.

SO THE STRUCK EAGLE STRETCHED UPON THE PLAIN

To have swept upward
past startled hands, past
frightened fingers, past bars, past
the idea of liberty even,
to have swept up
out of this iron Egypt, this winter day
was this coincidence?
                By acting now on the external world
                and changing it,
                he at the selfsame time
                changes his nature.

OFFICIOUS HASTE DID LET TOO SOON THE SACRED EAGLE FLY

In the prison
of the underworld,
in Sheol (Tropicana),
their spectrum of colors
spreads the radiance of Egypt
for the golden bull
and his spangled heifer.

In the 19th century,
from Bogotá, Colombia,
millions of hummers p.a.
One London firm alone:
400,000 corpses
plucked for adornment.

FOR WHERESOEVER THE CARCASE IS THERE WILL THE EAGLES BE GATHERED
 TOGETHER

Though the people do not even flock to their king.
It is enough that the king rules again
wingtip to wingtip spanning the upper air
and clouding the nether air with his shadow.
All those these walls enthrall, while more
than mathematic gloom envelops all around,
peer up from city windows and compute
the king's position in the famished skies.

The gates of Sheol
open on corridors
which open onto light
in this our world. But that illusion,
quantum of darkness in the rush of light,
bars hummers from the knowledge of their freedom.
Egypt is weariness of heart. Specifications of
    319 Apodiformes Trochilidae:
    flight muscles forming
    some 25% of body weight,
    unique wingbone to shoulder swiveljoint
    permits wingplane adjustment to the air.
    55 wingbeats per second in hoverflight,
    75 w.p.s. in level flight. Courtship:
    (O as for U-loop love-buzz) 200 w.p.s.

SKYWARD IN AIR A SUDDEN MUFFLED SOUND THE DALLIANCE OF EAGLES

While the king has not learned his trade.
Who shall, from the holarctic rim, in legions,
as in the days of Aquila Chrysaëtos, hoist in Rome,

bate bearing crowns and scepters in their pinions,
lightning in talons, the blizzard in their tails,
flutter'd your Volscians in Corioli,
and teach to kill? and teach to wind
the kingdom out on ever widening orbits?

The list of his Majesty's subjects
in his provinces of latter-day Egypt:
Cuban Bee, Calypte Helenae, 2½ in., Isle of Pines.
Frilled Coquette, Lophornis Magnifica, 2¾ in., Brazil.
Adorable Coquette, Paphosia Adorabilis, 3 in., Costa Rica.
Popelaire's Thornbill, Popelairia Popelairii, 4½ in., Ecuador.
Violet Sabrewing, Campylopterus Hemileucurus, 5 in., Mexico-Panama.
Collared Inca, Coeligena Torquata, 5½ in., Colombia-Peru.
Sappho Comet, Sappho Sparganura, 7 in., Bolivia.
Greentailed Sylph, Aglaiocercus Kingi, 7½ in., Andes.
Crimson Topaz, Topaz Pella, 7½ in., Guianas.
Streamertail, Trochilus Polytmus, 9½ in., Island of Jamaica.
                    And others as per itemized list attached.

Here in Sheol
by skeletal willows,
by ghostly streams,
their exiled harps are hung.
They doze in hibernation by the hour.
Their king has gone out of bondage from Egypt,
Babylon, Spain, New Spain and all the Russias.
                    Ring'd with the azure world he stands,
                    And the best of merry luck to him.

THAT WITH HIS SHARPE LOK PERSETH THE SONNE

While the king has not learned his trade.
He addresses, fratres, the flanneled crowd, Romani,
the keepers and dogs, populares, he addresses,
the city truants, workers, the photographers, of the world,
the journalists, unite, he addresses, the Sunday idle,
every valley, scorning the ladders, shall be exalted,
or baited lures, and every mountain shall be laid low,
the other dainty captives brought to tempt him,

he addresses, comfort ye, his tormentors, comfort ye,
dropping away, my people, with one flap of his leathers.

Toward Sheol
as toward
a fear to find, within the body's watch,
the jeweled bone responsibility,
they are content, in cages wide as breath,
wide as breath only, to spring the adequate
and whip their whirring wings from sip to song.
          Crests, fans, tufts, wires, pendants and
          pantaloons, shields, gorgets, whiskers,
          and irridescent plumage. Nature
          plus History will shortly be as one.

THE WRENS MAKE PREY WHERE EAGLES DARE NOT PERCH

Beyond these walls, this stone circumference,
lie his enthusiasms, snow-pure, untampered with,
ready to leap-frog time. Which, born in slavery,
he has not learned to scan. Here where the earth is glue
and feeds but stubble he dreams an Israel,
the rocks and crags on which he builds his nest,
the heart of cedars where he plants his banners,
the dove-gray prey so hot of blood, the sun
crazing the day, the soothing moon,
the taloned stars: Sheol in splinters.

The hummer never walks or climbs. Feet are
for perching only. Metabolism rate
being so high, migrations of
500 miles would call
for subcutaneous fuel loads
adding 50% to body weight
before the Exodus.
          Lab tests have proved
          such feats impossible.
          Yet hummers could
          back in their days of Nature,
          before the massacres and slaughters

(tears of the Indies)
perform it nonetheless twice every year.

THAT IS THE HUM-BIRD NOT MUCH EXCEEDING A BEETLE

Wherefore the king, as all such stories end, will learn
his trade. His shadow magnifies the swelling land,
stooping to prey grown fat on idleness.
He has gone to Pharaoh who said No. He has decided Yes.
He has worked out that frontiers concern subjects
who may rot in their colors and emblems if they will.
He will shift continents, change poles, night into day, day, night.
Freeze deserts, make of the sands his snows.
Fire the snows, renew himself in ice.
Quit his armies if need be and resign after Canaan.

Though the city change coin into weapons, and ingots
to instruments of war, his lungs will flower, his heart
bear fruit. Mounting up with wings as a storm cloud, unafraid.
That the seas may not run dry, nor the rivers falter.

Burying his right wing in orchards and vineyards
against the whirlwind bred on Sinai,
honey lapped from a lion gut, milk from the mouths of lambs,
men lie with beaks and talons, marrow for talismans,

where they shall not fear, naked bone, but for him in his air,
in this crucible's fire, a throne, a torch of spices —
in the fan of his wings now, his resurrected voice,
the assent of these palms, in this wind, peace,

nor shall there be slaves anymore. Peace. Selah. Poem. Amen.

october

THE CURTAINS

The leaves are coming down
the walls of my life
      are not more solid

I hear the leaves coming down
at night   they make the noise of footsteps
or the kisses of children
they fall like a curtain
      between the leaves
bits of a sky we try to remember

"There was in that man
had he been left unshaken by his stars
      a happy disposition"

On the other side of the curtain
the fathomless country lies about us
the farms
      sitting like loaves among the fields
the animals
      at home in their own breaths
needing no byres
      and birds never a roost

We have seen it
  we know it by heart
      men of no season

I shall build on nothing
on nothing build my house
out of the iron nail   remorselessly
hammered into the ground of this dead year

the nail   so bald   so cold
out of humiliation and the grinding feet
on nothing build my house
and when the leaves are fallen
and hammering is done
the curtains of the house will have been hung

Through which we glimpse
the place we shall inhabit
        full void   that memory

THE PICTURES

Certain Octobers
ran with blood
as if the sun had touched the earth
and turned its rivers to blood
ours is a quiet time needing to build

I had never been a young poet
those dreams of entering a room   smiling
turning the head this way and that   bowing
taking a perfumed hand
leading the most beautiful away to the waltz

"You have an openness around the eyes
that shows a willingness to learn and to accept
the new experience   with this you cannot age"

The pictures dream in an empty hall
the figures in the pictures dream
their heads thrown back   with throats exposed
to knives of light   a ceiling falling
our hesitations touch each other

I dream they are calling me
the young faces eager for what I have to say
I've not yet found the way to say it

Our shoulders rub together
we sketch desire inside us with our hands
we are given
moments   a succession of moments
when shall we get
                       time we ask
uninterrupted time
and still more time when conversation fails
exhausted talk drifting from our mouths
like mist

                  and perhaps sleep
the satisfaction of silence

There should be
a society for the protection of
the deeply married

THE DARK NIGHT

Perhaps the most terrible thing about la noche oscura
is that it comes about in broad daylight

My life has moved out of me and taken possession
of territories I have not mapped
I walk by myself   empty and wondering
where this or that has been misplaced

If once I wanted to lay the world
and all my salvages
at somebody's feet
that desire is now done with

Someone must return all I've lost to me
and feed me to my prime
I shall be rich and give away treasure
allowed to proceed another few years

Not long ago I marched through cities
for something better than we have
though the details elude me
There was some question in my mind
of rediscovering a fire   some youth
some fire for myself would also cease to burn
children I did not love but others loved as I
can sometimes love my children

and cities were littered with banners
black and red flags   the writing on the wall
the ashes of old fires we carry in ourselves
we covered much asphalt and green grass

Above our heads   in a misted sky
the shape of branches made a trellis against the sun
"—somewhere there is a country where no leaves fall—"
consumed in its own light

and on the branches   birds of paradise
spun like raucous fireworks with long tail feathers
in a world we had never reached   any of us
in a light we had never seen burning

THE WORDS

The ground   takes all the leaves
in autumn's gift
and raises other trees for other seasons

Those who are going down into themselves
on every page of every newspaper
seeping away under our sullen noses

their catalog should be as bare
as a fall's trees
the names saying no more
no less than branches

We have not blood enough
to agonize with Viets
another day Biafrans
another day the Czechs

the lovely tribes   falling like shadows

If we must play with words
the nouns should be like lungs
sooted with smoke
the verbs like cancers   ravaging the blood

Where is the life I lead
how dare I lead it
how shall the earth survive
endless attrition

the flies are falling from the leaves
our words will soon be pared
to a single sound

THE JOINING OF HANDS

Our hands   unable to touch
our fingers begin to think
we work across landscapes
        thick with impediments
I begin to walk through you
        you walk through me for a while
coming upon clear prairies
        and then we are retrieved

Sleepwalking in the streets
crossing a bridge
as if we were to couple
        among the roots of trees
I've laid our freedom on this town
        a map   a grid
and the sea has rushed in
        to drown intelligence

In the poem I give you my hands
where you will sense
their joining overhead
        give me the birds of summer
beyond intelligence
        for they know ways in air
far countries where we need not meet
        married already there

In the poem I give you my hands

        you cannot lose

THE SILENCE

I am a silent place
yes   look   I have done it now
the birds migrate through me
the leaves peel off my bones
the seasons drop their privacies
        undress through me

I am a listening place for your ears
where you can hear the sea as in a shell
        and all its languages
now there is an island in the sea
now there are birds on the trees
        the falling leaves reveal the birds

I flow through this town   the traffic flows
round my escarpments   my retreat
I am the guest of this town
it is feeding me
limbs   smiles   a thousand faces
        I talk to none of them

and yet   where the birds fly
out of my cast-off clothes
where I dare and am dared in the silence
there is never more than a breath
to draw between gain and loss
        yes   of all the world

and he approaches me
the sinner of a moment ago
his mouth sick with a swarm of flies

but the birds are free of vermin
flying through me
and the carpet of leaves is clean

the beautiful contradictions

In Memoriam Charles Olson and Hugh MacDiarmid

ONE

To cease working in shadow with the light against us
no longer concerned with the fate of any particular element
thrashing to emerge from swaddling cloths
since the problem is to love all without loss of edge
from particular   the uses of   to general   the uses of
to work in the naked light with elation   extreme elation

and once the experiment has begun to make an end of it
so that no frontiers whatsoever be accredited
with heart and mind agreed on the minimal solutions
necessary for each individual to live under a roof
with clean air   clean food   clean water   clean time to use
working in open light   elated   hard   sharp   put it diamond-like   for

it is a myth you know that desire dissolves all obstacles
it has never been known to dissolve mountains at all
and should the most violent fire you can imagine melt one
nevertheless another would grow up precisely in the same place
and the landscape look exactly the same as it did before
because there is no end to the production and destruction of mountains

This is the discipline required of us now
whether we have   or not   any chance of success
we have no alternative to taking the whole world as our mother
since no one can pretend to own anything of permanence
or to anchor his roots in any particular plot
or speak in anything but borrowed languages

Every time we arrive at a new place
we grope around in it as roots must grope in the earth
look for the detail will seem to make us its owner
but by the time the leaves turn away from the sun
we have almost forgotten the tongue we spoke to break silence
our origin holes are covered with stones

Tell us this mountain is no longer the tallest of mountains
the tree-lines have moved up or down so many hundred feet
say these grass plains have become a desert
this trail has not been walked in living memory
the last of these animals laid itself down before our birth
these are no longer our boundaries

Nevertheless we recite the old world because we own it in our souls
and when we tell its places in their proper order
we are sickened to death by the illusions men have about mine and thine
the skin we wear having been designed to fit each one of us
and never for a moment tailored to mask any particular race
the covenant hacked out of it once and for all   the flesh saved

It is up to me   since I must lose myself   to call them one by one
wearing these tattered fragments of the human skin
to persuade them that from time to time they must think of filial duties
such as bringing the relics together at the cremation pyre
drawing a human shape on a piece of ground
lying still in the waters surrounded with light

I shall have to pass through every birth   every occasion of birth

                    so that the river turn of its own accord

the waters run back to break
                              out from her all at once

it is up to me to call into being everything there is

FOUR

My job she told us   with some solemnity
is to lift the myth like a bandage from his eyes
to show him that only in imagination have I ever been his mother
(mother-marriage won't work in theory and is bound to be rough in practice
we don't marry our mothers   sisters   daughters   because
we exchange them for other men's women)
so look I said she told us   stop looking at me this way if you can
to show him that only in imagination had I ever been his mother
but made small progress

He had never set eyes on a woman before   had gone on hearsay
to guess those breasts a trifle ripe now signaled me the creature
marching up that mountain spiral martially as he did
and me so cold lying there for the vultures to defile
the circle of fire about me as useless as a bathroom heater
his eyes were closed   I'd say he was dreaming just as I was dreaming
who had prophesied his birth in his real mother's womb
before my father kissed the splendor off my eyes
so how *could* we be the same woman for heaven's sake   and yet

I wonder whether we're ever going to have some breakfast in the Ring
eggs and bacon at sunrise   for instance   or have to leave the room
(both possibilities to ease an audience into sympathy)
Why not a production on those lines without the long discussions
the singers going through a day at home from rise to lie me down
with breakfast and sitting in real toilets if need be
all that very much of course while they sing
because it is a myth you know that desire dissolves all obstacles
while feeding and singing keep our figures redundant

    i.   He kills his father on the way up the mountain
    ii.   he sees a woman killed by his father
    iii.   seeing a woman for the first time he is surprised and thinks her mother
    iv.   she has to dissuade him but he is not really fooled
    v.   they agree that the unreality of art is unreliable
    vi.   he blinds himself in the traditional manner
    vii.   her breasts soak his feet in milk

viii.   he treads his milk into hers
 ix.   at the top of the stairs all her mouths open to sing

I say he blinded himself because he began to guess I'm not the one
as I stood at the top of the stairs he received me entirely
received me like a host and devoured me
from the top of the stairs I looked down at him and laughed
with the whole of his god in his mouth
all my doors were opening to give out food and drink
I was feeding the needy and comforting the sick
far beyond the circle of the burning mountain
the fields began to warm again under a blanket of harvests

Perhaps he knew that he had to go blind in order to speak
with any pretence at prophecy
to tell his own youth of the marriage it had contracted
on that dusty crossroads where the gods were waiting
he goes down now into everything his mother once made
out there among the fields where plants grow by her virtue
no one will ever mine the coal in her eyes
the diamonds glisten on her singing throat
she gives its birth to everything there is

            by our father's will I am made his bride

FIVE

Looking into the eyes of babies in experiments
born without the normal pressure on their skulls
thinking they are going to put an end to philosophy
when some development of this begins to breed monsters
and that the chase through probability of the genius
the great kick he gives through his mother as he comes out
the clarity of the air surrounding him later in life
however much his body might take revenge on him
his mind crack between the diameter of his skull and the crown

reality comprises

that the immeasurable heave of the whole race
to bring this animal to the tree's crest and enthrone him there
may be gone forever in a moment of medical history
like the passing of some art   or an old migration
of all the birds together in the arms of the same wind
the way the planet used to turn in one direction with one purpose

frightens a lot

I remember on the shores of the most beautiful lake in the world
whose name in its own language means abundance of waters
as if the volcanos surrounding it had broken open the earth
there in the village of Saint James of Compostela one cold night
not the cereus-scented summer nights in which a voice I never traced
sang those heartbreaking serenades to no one known
a visiting couple gave birth in the market place
the father gnawing the cord like a rat to free the child
and before leaving in the morning they were given the freedom of the place

I mean the child was given

FIFTEEN

The elders at the zenith of their power look down the sky
from the decline of the mountain   the ocean slide
the homeward slope   an uninhabited moon
in the path of the westering sun   their hair shining
theirs is forgetfulness   intermittent recognition
remembrances of youth greatly outnumbering recent events
they look down with patience mostly

they range the empty desert   they are few and far between
they go back into the dream companionless
they sit for hours on end throwing their shadows on time
their blood spurts into the earth they worship
they urinate into dishes to mix their paints
their saliva and snot go into gum for a few tools
with which they keep the earth in movement

If I had not waited for all the bricks to be baked in the kilns
for the measurements of the house to be laid out on plans
if I had not thought of improvements time after time
not given way to desire for larger establishments
with more impressive gardens   a greater variety of flowers
if I had not insisted day in day out on the need for construction above all
if I had recognized the imperfection of created things

and made no more than a living room with table   chair   pen
paper in the table drawers   variable weather on the panes
I would have salvaged much of the life I have slept away
for no matter how long the years at our disposal
how often do we feel for any lasting moment
that we are inhabited by the exact voice of what we need to say
not riding alongside   but upon our voice

You have probably known also the desire to be free of these bones
this envelope of skin   this skin sail full of wind
you have probably wanted to fill your beds with as many lovers as could be
        heard
above the din of individual love
you have been the curators of your own properties
filled your house with goods that will not talk back
tried to collect the uncollectable world

and yet I am not so sure that this desire to encompass all is vanity
it may be the only effort most of us are allowed to make at wisdom
for if rightly understood the balance of this universe is perfect
there is not a hairbreadth of distinction between our good and our evil
though there be room enough to die when feet tread dreams
I accept the imperfection of man   the impurity of action now
allow it all to come at me in its almost unbearable complexity

let it be my task   my pride   to ride it out like breakers
let me be at its mercy like a swimmer in water   a bird on the wind
that my arms   my wings   might twist and turn in the weathers
let me trust that the sum of our imperfections is the body of justice
whose mould squats in the empty desert awaiting our return
let us lay down our single flowers   coffin them down together
let their fruit be ground again   let there be new seed

Among all who cut the knot in the name of sanity   of progress
among the ever more busy hives   the ever proliferating systems
without which this planet cannot take its place in the concourse of planets
who then   charged with the task of preserving language
in this babel of dialects where none has the desire to legislate anymore
but only blindly and efficiently to follow the conventions of his task
shall discriminate   select   unite the corpus of law   if not the poet

being acknowledged at last as maker among makers   master of dialectic
rhyming the fields and cities   scanning the roads
apportioning the harvests   liberating the days
motor of energies   guide of hands   bed of rest
setting his songs to music   his music to the spheres
he has time in the earth his body   he has time to spare
for the most beautiful revolution of all

being acknowledged at last   master of dialectic
when this is going to be a unity of which you have no conception as yet
the earth will have gone over the horizon for good into the stars
the one on one love of men and women be an indulgence of the past
we shall be half fish   a quarter bird   something of animals in love
though keeping the root of man   reclassify the angels among the planets
remember our past lives   set out our futures in their frames

there shall be no separation anymore between parents and offspring
the leap-frog generations   the interminable execution of fathers
the suffering of mothers donating sons in war
the anguish of younger brothers unprepared to take their elders' places
the giving away of brides to the holocaust
the offer of children to fire in the streets
the milking of human seed to perpetuate the races

The prophet finds it impossible to live for he who predicts in time
robs himself of his own present and what shall I make of my life
who have brought it to this point in time   to this place
where shall I meet with my existence   where encounter it
among what bones can we come to terms with each other   my death and I
shall I be standing at the door after all those years still ignorant
of how I got there in the first place   still unready to go in

with what voice shall I describe the ceremony of passing out of this
        incarnation
looking down upon myself in peace a fourscore-year man
the great worm may writhe in his hole in the center of the stage
the hero who passed me earlier and transfixed me with his spear
may fight body to body with it   overcome it to birdsong
with the seductive smile   the very smile I had around his age
before going to find his bride on the burning mountain

where do I tell you the secrets a lifetime has stored for you
where can I speak to you face to face if not here
as I prepare to sing out the praises of created things
completely forgetting what cannot be said on their behalf
The rooms of my life grow wide
in all their corners there is room to breathe   there are windows
my house is built upon the labyrinths   the mazes of the worm

I have known the worm too in my time   the worm is not alien to me
I have had the worm in my guts for most of my life
there is no distinction to be made between species of worm
the worm has paraded up and down in me twisting his cocky head
in my childhood science was ignorant   tests always negative
in my maturity society too careless   I writhed daily of the worm
I am a corridor through which the worms pass and take their ease

the worm does not wait for my death to go in and come out of me
he finds his solace in my bed   he makes his breeding ground
he promenades in and out of the bodies of my wife and children
passing from one person to another at a touch of the fingers
almost it seems he passes at the glance of an eye
the worm multiplies in my house as I have less and less years to keep
this is how he lives off me   I do no more than house him

yet I welcome his passage and the beautiful contradictions of his work
the lichen of excrement he leaves in me that excretes him in due time
as a denominator of the flights that we all take through one another
the most material sign of certain processes   some of which are of spirit
All of a sudden life is very beautiful
there is an everbloom at the center of my existence
I want life to go on for ever

among the blossoms of this floribunda which has forgotten seasons
each of whose individual flowers sucks the paps of justice one by one
as they hang from the bosom of the sky
there is a fruit for each one of you I encounter on my path
and one for each one that I do not encounter
we shall all meet one day on a long lawn   at the age of eighty
and talk over tea or drinks why we did not love each other more

There is a lady in blue with red hair going through a garden in Seurat
she is surrounded with a light of green and blue
she carries a parasol that says everything about the uses of paint
she has collected us together   herded our offerings
she shepherds our lights along in dabs of color
she goes to meet her lover with our souls in her skirts
I think she may be the bride of God going back to her husband

we are her sons here looking up the sky along our white beards
we have waited a long time for her to go back to him
it is strange that we are so much older than she appears to be
as we see her walking with her free hand tucking her gown
toward the husband that has never been painted in any picture
through the rows of multicolored flowers we can no longer number
we can think of no questions for her anymore   nothing we wish her to ask

a nowhere for vallejo

M.S.

(A)

"Yo nací un día
que Dios estuvo enfermo
grave"
—LOS HERALDOS NEGROS

Conch shells at Mass
        alcaldes standing   golden cloaks
staffs tipped with silver
        alpaca lining   shield   flocks on their knees

priest dropping shards for the thousandth time
        of shattered language
the sacristan distributes herbs of grace
        and lights to the village elders

as   suddenly
            the church roof sails
                        several feet into the air
the Sun opens its arms

the risen Host covers the face of the Sun like a kerchief
        and the wild thrones bellow
                    dominations howl
archangels blare

                a poet   born
from the depths of the sea
                in Santiago de Chuco
on the scar of Peru

and female the soul of the absent one
and female my very own
till when shall we be waiting for
what no one owes us

People at the door outside
        press in against the temple
cheeks to their fathers' stones
                    cave in like the walls of the sea

Sad destiny not to have ever lived   but dead forever
        being dry leaf   unknown to green
                orphan of orphans
                        and

Mother   I go tomorrow to Santiago
                to wet me in your benediction and your tears

A child of seven
        ravished by the fiesta procession
especially   the standard-bearer
        racing home to his mother

Mother   I want to be the standard-bearer

Conch shells at Mass
        alcaldes gathered at the door
shrunk in the light of flash-bulbs
a girl throwing petals on the vicar's head   he shrugs them off

I shall come back to Peru when not one stone is left standing

I

*"Tal la tierra oirá en tu silenciar
cómo nos van cobrando todos
el alquiler del mundo donde nos dejas
y el valor de aquel pan inacabable"*
— TRILCE

And they went down into the king-city
Tahuantinsuyu   four-quarters   limbs of man
                    to find the skull

happening there   first thing   on the poet's name
who'd become such a hero to his country
                    though he had left it
they'd finally put up a statue in the square
                    fronting the church of famine

and he walked up to the monument
                    and kissed the poet's name
with his hand

In "La Langouste Selon Désir"
he heard the wind going through her tears
the bird feeding its young in the myth
opened its breast   blood flowing out
                    flapped lazily over city and harbor
catch of fish   dying children

Bird-glider over the city
wall-wings   oven-beak
falls on the statue of the caesar-poet
                    bread on the sea

Where they buy and sell a country
            we were talking about the dead with the rich
eating their platos criollos
                    in "The House of the Thirty Coins"

talking with the satellite vendors
               with which the country we don't know
listens to the one we do

In a city full of movement
with the woman he loves
crying for the caesar-poet to come back
               and eat them alive one by one
the friends   the enemies
                              eat them all
in words born and dead at this table

and then a constant
        quiet
murmur about gold

he hears the wind going through her tears
her tears   the queen-city
married a king with her hair in his eyes
above the grave of the caesar-poet

he feeds the children crying in her tears

II

"Es el tiempo este anuncio de gran zapatería
es el tiempo que marcha descalzo
de la muerte   hacia   la muerte"
— POEMAS HUMANOS

Call of green things to his hand
        no longer pulls
underworld gold
pales for his lack of envy

The things of poverty
        he sees as clear
as mountain teeth
        about to bite the sky
as the backbone of mountains
        about to puncture the sky's belly

The city is gray with white hands
        the city
                the city
is gray with white   and green   hands
        beckons the forests
cold mountain's reaches

They say the same mists will come down
        but be drunk by the Sun
they say there will be a Sun up there
        but it will be cold

Old man in a brown hat
        drip at his nose
passing
the eyes   /   of a door through mountains
one way
        with no thought of return

Frozen to gold
            demonetized gold
to be dug up at dawn
            changed into mountains

Wind on the sands   cat-god   mouse
            mouse on cat   cat on mouse
lovers lying side by side in the mountains
                        he is about to enter

Her oyster is the Moon's
            around it   a city
prayer in his hands
            calls to the caesar-poet

                    venture out there

And where are you
                macho
in all this sleep
                rotting about our bodies

Taken a bus twice only   these fifteen years

III

"Y preguntamos por el eterno amor,
por el encuentro absoluto,
por cuanto pasa de aquí para allá."
— TRILCE

In the Andean night
he saw her shed her skin and come out of herself
      as from a chrysalis   the walls of cunning
and she stood up above herself

a moth enjoying the wind

Her right hand went out   bearing an offering
her left hand also   at about the same height
      they took her for Justice discussing this country
night broke the balance   her feathered mouth

brushing their genitals   man after man

and those who had etched their names on her walls
a death's-head now   between her shoulder-blades
      fell   powder from her wings
onto the highroads of the continent

moth-dust on rolling tires

Aging priests on the plaza
dressed in the flesh she had worn before birth
      flayed god of sacrifice
dances   her pores will want to speak

and the people back away like Spring rain

He knows where she has lost the thread
of the myth they constructed together
      yet their life opens on down
she has no means of ever closing it

He said   he said   in the rush of air
        as sand blew in the maze
as the labyrinth silted up
                        that desert's name

(B)

"El valle es de oro amargo;
y el viaje es triste, es largo."
— LOS HERALDOS NEGROS

From mountains   in his eighteenth year
     to cloistered city   sea among its walls
initiated study   body   spirit
     about the time of Spring   about the resurrection
dropped out because of penury
     teaching the young what he had never learned
mid-year a time for travels
     the Fall   for action

Young well-to-do
     guns   hounds   and fighting cocks
closing their houses to all but the sea
     girls fail to pass his watches
a yellow billet in his yellow hands
     his verses made   out of the medievals
his spirit-kin   Rimbaud   and other French
     even in prison   prizes   competitions

And we would see him crossing
     the ficus-shaded streets
locked behind doors   washed in our rooms
     on our own solitudes
his garments black   a lion's mane
     black lion's mane   from cordilleras
always his elegance   each day a dandy
     his clothes with little work to do   upon those bones

Trujillo-Lima   elegant boats
   cold captain giving orders
I'll be the one who's gone
     until the boat for France   El Oroyo   third class
in a sad mid-June   where he would never rest
     before he'd died of Spain   like Garcilaso

Peruvian tongue   choked in its walls
        scum on colonial tides

And his loves   shut oysters
        betrayed to knives   numbered   outnumbered
love-speech to the roses of the coastal cities
        awash on sleep   the sleep of childhood
What are you doing now   my sweet   my Andine Rita
        of rushes   of capulli
her sex   a tomb   shut to the sea at last
        calls him in from the streets

After the fire   that night of chichas
        Darío singing   *las Américas celestes*
they were all of one mind to arrest him
        wherever found   for a dubious crime
the court long closed in that Pacific province
        far dying star of his youth
would harrow   extradite   imprison him   in dreams
        even in the city of light

They have taken a poet prisoner   Doctor Polar
        imagine   a poet prisoner
But that is inconceivable   Who is the poet
        The great poet Vallejo   Doctor Polar

Gravest time of my life   in a Peruvian jail

VIII

"En el muro de pie, pienso en las leyes
que la dicha y la angustia van trocando:"
— *LOS HERALDOS NEGROS*

Borders slide backward   forward
weak kings   lose a strong king's conquests
       Sun image on the mountain lakes
empire-provider   whether cold or hot
        reigns from the start of time

His train   a messenger
agonizes between the mountains
       at loss for a breath of air
through eye of rock
       into the mountain's skull

forward   then back   forward   then back
                forward again
locates a stream of air
          hardly dares breathe it

At four thousand five hundred   climbing
       passes out of earth's hold
out of its grasp and keep
       spine   transparent now
    snake vertebrae
     in a royal necklace
    eyes crystallized
          gone beyond darkness
     on the edge of light
      lungs failing
    sucking like bellows
     sight improving
all the time
   until at last he comes
a riveder le stelle

And he has seen
          gigantes   /   monstruos
teeth   prison bars
          gargantas   famine
dueños de los montes
          the archangelical
Michel et toute sa compagnie
               du temps de sa jeunesse
in his days of youth

Where Justice goes   puffs along tracks
          with her dimmed eyes
breasts   flanks of mountains
          purse-bellied after many children
and cleft of earthquake

Sun astride mountains   mail of gold

X

"ante el pesar de los padres de no poder dejarnos
de arrancar de sus sueños de amor a este mundo;"
— TRILCE

Passing the Palace of Justice
     a cab driver says
great deal of palace
         for so little justice

Photographers in rain
their cameras backed up
storks at the Station wall
      trapped in their own last portraits

Where they mine his ores
     wrecks of better housing
         in the high towns
there are no gardens
     children tell homes apart
by numbers on the blocks
         Arbeit macht frei

Noses stuffed against dust
     on the prowl for their lungs
whole babies under shawls
     stifle in mother smell
while guts torn up
     golden wombs opened
give up their treasures
       puffing down to the coast

The wounded country
     whose past is drained
by vampire and vulture
     out of whose wounds
torrent of ore
     angry and sick

such men have drained
    to add their own blood to the torrent

And the caesar-poet
    walks in far Paris his night-walk
exhausted by Justice
        as he falls to his drink
cats lap the blood
    of the land he recovers in dreams

His fathers   from the hills
    look down erosion
try tracing paths
        messengers traveled
to bring news of the Sun
                    bread to his children

    smouldering arms to the mines

(D1)

"Empiezo a reconocer en la suma miseria mi vía
auténtica y única de existencia."
— VALLEJO TO PABLO ABRIL. XII.XI.MCMXVII

In the same way   suffered most cautiously
thus not to cry or weep   since eyes themselves
have   independently of self   their poverties
          I mean to say   their functions
                              something
that skids from soul   and falls to soul

                    Orphan of language
                    orphan of orphancies
                    black debt in Paris
                    disdain in Lima
                    To do no more than die
                    need death at every moment

Pablo   there are in life
hours of a black   closed blackness
shut to all consolation
          hours more sinister   I'd say
more awesome than the tomb

                    I do not know
                    the paths that lead to comfort
                    to happiness
                    have never taken them
                    Thus all is well   very well as it is
                    and above all   in essence

This child's facility for tears
sunk in huge pity for all things
remembering my fathers   often   dear ones lost
          One day   I shall manage to die
in the hazardous life I've had to carry

and then   as now
you'll witness me
minus encouragement
or almost any love
I have no present
or for that matter   future

And if   after so many words
the word itself failed to survive
and if   after bird wings
the bird at rest   failed to survive
        Better in truth   "eat" everything   and finish

                    And as for politics
                    I've gone according to
                    the proper weight of all things
                    Understand me Juan   one lives one's life
                    as it enters into him
                    almost always   by way of surprise

As I go on living
life teaching me
I am getting much clearer about ideas and feelings
relative to the matters and men of America
        It seems to me   we need great fury
        and a terrible destructive impulse for everything
        to be found in those places
        One must destroy   and destroy oneself
This can't go on   must not go on
Since we have no leaders to rely on
we must unite   at least   in a tight bundle
of wounded and furious people
        burst out   tearing to pieces
        all things around us   or in our power
Above all   we must destroy ourselves
and afterward   the others
        Without the prior sacrifice of self
        there is no possible salvation

Leaving les flics   in the andine air
                of Paris town   the poet said
We owe life nothing now
                and have the right to be happy

Everything's happy   except my happiness

REQUIEM PRO DUABUS FILIIS ISRAEL

In memoriam: Assia & Shura

". . . et perducant te in civitatem sanctam Jerusalem.
Chorus angelorum te suspiciat et cum Lazare quondam
paupere aeternam habeas requiem.
Requiem aeternam dona eis, Domine: et lux perpetua luceat eis."

The trees proffer their leaves
                    she is not here
the birds prepare to mate
                    she keeps no company
the roads are bright with traffic festivals
the wings of windows laze on singing air
the earth ages another day
                 another day
                     another day

she will not age
                  she does not see it
she is no witness to
                the celebration

and our days have died   there is no energy
in hand or foot   the brain is dull
thought starved before it comes to birth
the dream locked in our minds   tedium destroying
                      all our occasions

Some weary angel took its eyes off her
turning its pinions from a faded sun
one moment
                  and she side-slipped into
silence   and speechlessness

Ruth in reverse
Boaz asleep under so many trees
after his work in many different fields

she was confused   wanting to follow
into closed regions he would not allow
into his languages
whose syllables were dark   whose phrases   dark
destroyed the very messages they carried her
his myth not hers   nor could it ever be
while unbeknown to her   all ships had foundered
all harbors drained into the sea
all trace of any home she could have had
erased from memory

With lungs still full of gas
with nostrils bruised by her last breath
she lies oak-packaged on a pedestal;
beside her   in white cloth
the child she took into the oven with her
after the crude excitement
the unexpected scandal
that was not done to call for any poem
now all her parts
committed to the fire
her crown of hair   first   and her hidden hair
under her arms   and hair between her thighs
and hair along the limbs   since she was dark
born of a foreign sun   and then the flesh
the hard flesh of the hands   the silk of inner limbs
down through the muscle   melting   down the reluctant bone
past a small yelp of soul
to the still ash   transmuted excrement

Now those are busy who will set her down
that language might survive
now some write literary history
some see her snared in myth
also themselves   the good she does for them
some write their in memoriams
and I this requiem
whose tongue could then have summoned
                    had I been so required
the hiss and vowel of her family

Daughter of daughter in the founding line
these daughters of the people gone   confused
the alien language squatting on our tongues
while from the coffin her clear cry for help
participation   and a place to sleep
in death's white syllables goes misunderstood
we give her up now   to the lapping fire
to Terezin   Auschwitz   and Buchenwald
for laziness   for emptiness of spirit

As tight as love   in the first days of love
romance unlived with her   as tight as love
the mind so tight   no other thought can slip
into the tight circumference
                              the moment blasted
each moment blasted in the thought of her
                              firstborn among the dead
when we no longer find the time to die
and   soon   will never need to

Beyond all blessings   hymns   praises   and consolations
that may be uttered in this world again
and say   Amen

Oseh shalom bim'romov
Hu ya-aseh shalom
oleinu v'al kol Yisroeil

V'imru Omein

THE GREAT ODOR OF SUMMER

To: David Lenfest

The land has been dead in its pores   all the war long
now wakes to dogwood   without transition
we've had no time at all for Spring
great perfume exhalations on the edges of Summer
fast water births and blood-filled afterbirths
the gloat of trees   leaf legions shining
trash of bird squadrons   animal regiments
coursing of eagles through clouds   freeing the scents
needles of warbler beaks in the clouds opening avenues
            for the freshening rain

        High on sleep   high on our own desires
            to the high scream of jays   their presages
        taking over these fields from the predators
            our own authority returning to our hands
        high on sleep   high over arguments
            messages   codes   informations
        listening to the say-so of time
            South Carolina talking the other day

        of the line which is the circle which is the line
            while more inches than needed were to lie down in Ohio

and in the trees the leaves were opening to a music
    not only the trees were to hear
seeds were preparing their shadows
    not only for generations of birds
and warblers were weaving round thick trunks
    a female lure to our preparations
            to perfume the reddening rain

        In a small corner of the dreamtime
            I dreamed the ceremony I had not seen on the first field
        those many days ago in the abundance of waters
            it was the pendant rite of bringing in the Summer

ah the rain   we had talked of that   had practiced that
        except that here the colors were as bright
as hay and corn and cardinals
and the brown of an infant's shit
    the war-chief had looked up at me sideways
        my presence worried him
    and the peace-chief too   holding his kite
        with which he was about to tie the earth
    to outer suns   to stars
they decided to carry out the rites
                        just as I woke
    in a corner of the dream
                            between hut and hut

and in her thickets   in her lowest reaches
where revolution slips   in her red placenta
we look to find in the bent-over branches
        the paradisal forking of desire
these odors of her effluence   her loving pollution
love's yielding form as yet unknown
        to all our lunge and parry in the dark

    I came to poetry late
        had looked to other things for my family
    and woke to find myself an orphan to all else
            then came my mother-fathers
        brothers   sisters   cousins
    sons   daughters   grandchildren   as thick as sand
        in the shape of other poets
    whose books I kissed
        as precisely as I would kiss a stone
    on falling in love with its polish

Warblers' wings like mouths brushing against the dark
butterflies panting   wet cunts of violets
        worms in the slime of the moon
the sun's hair streaming
        bent to our roots as our heads batter the skies
            to break the gathering dark

Well
What will you do with the Academy?
saw down the branch you sit on?
transform it?   burn it?   rape it?
drown it in wine and sperm?
dance it to ritual?
retrieve it for disaster?
fruitful disaster?
take it over for your own harvest?
occupy the great odor?

When we sit down to talk of values
and start where most men end
neglecting the simple beginnings
we make an end of the Academy
I am interested in those who begin at the beginning
philosophers in caves   playing with light and shadow
taking the explanations of others who sit in caves
and welding them together into one answer
Look   do you know
that 99% of mankind is syncretistic
that isms are a luxury of the rich
and that we
with our eyes of ice
our eyes of petal and flame
our eyelids like the wings of summer flies
in the great light of total opposition

are poor   and rightly poor   and rightly   rightly   poor?

And Beatrice   if she had lived
what then?
if she'd been met with   at every corner
by the poet at his work
or at his meditations
if she had walked with that sweet front of hers to the wind
like an aging revolution with banners
her hair against the sharp horizon of her wings
with rhetoric on her upper lip
and the booty of war on the lower?

No   the muse dies
            to the high cry of jays
the muse ages
                    she changes altogether
                        the muse dies
            to the high omen of jays in the cut-up of the Summer sky
                    and we start another revolution
                    our authority returns to us
                    in the great odor of Summer
                    in the freshness of our own days

The small blue world in my hand
                        like an eye I have lost
I glare at with the other eye
                        the small blue world
running with blood   prepared for you
            while we select the America we are dreaming
and the great elegy that the world is writing for itself
                        in silence somewhere
            hardly known to itself
which we recite behind our voices   each time we speak

To the Academy in the tundra   to the Academy in the forest
to the Academy in the fields   to the Academy in the marshes
to the Academy in the mountains   to the Academy in the clouds
to the Academy in the rivers   to the Academy in the seas
to the Academy of love   to the Academy of pleasure
to the Academy of beauty   to the Academy of desire
to the Academy of surprise   to the Academy of imagination

            to the blood on our pavements   and on the bayonets
            to the blood on the brain's gutters   on the heart's canals
            to the blood on our hands   and in our armpits
            to the blood in our eyes   and in our matted hair
            to the blood over this field as over Ohio
            we subscribe   high on sleep   high on our own awaking
            under the scream of jays   in the great odor of Summer

                                                    v.v. mcmlxx

                                        .

68

the persephones

For P.R.T.

THE FIFTH PERSEPHONE

When they came for her to the land of the many
when she had been located in the land of
he who receives the many/
                and the father of all
had agreed to her return two seasons out of three
he slipped her the seed of darkness as a
                pomegranate
which she ate out of violence and without agreement
                for her freedom.

                The ruin of herself
entered her like a mist, it was as if
her prime stood against the sky like a palace
the palace of the kings with all its towers
its battlements and her age
to its peak of perfection there, all banners flying.
And any onlooker could have told the perfection
the peak of perfection about to crest
in those breaking towers.

                And any singer could have told
with eloquence that she had reached her peak
had never been lovelier with that mist inside her
but she also would have known
                that from now on
there was no path but down
                and that come winter in the land above
she'd fall to shades she ruled by right
and by the gravity of her accomplishments.

                Meanwhile the mother
in the city of her mysteries every night in the fire
held the king's child in the fire to make him ageless
to make him immortal little by little, the lovely prince.
She drank no wine, but only barley and rye water,
she stood in doorways with her head to the ceiling
filling the doorway with a divine light and men with fear,

she wore dark veils like clouds masking her ageless beauty
and had given up the company of her own kind.

     She did not grieve for those perfections
brought to fulfillment in the daughter but only men grieved
who had seen death enter her body and didn't know how to hack out
the roots of loss which had gripped her heart.

THE NINTH PERSEPHONE

"J'ai quitté toute ma terre . . ."

She goes into the dark
    out of the flowers into the singing machines
which grind her down through the earth to her rightful home—

    having spoken in the world above
    with the king of light
          with the image
    of he who receives the many
          turned into light
these conversations her whole peace
         her gratitude
    her dues to what remains of the season

the old modes
        serenities
           foundations of her throne
in the kingdom of the unborn children and the born
her mother's pride among the irises
the fountains made of people who had wept out their lives
         in search of happiness

which is what, this happiness, which is what this possession,
self-possession, other-possession, thing-possession,
the bringing together of what belongings, what ideas,
what visions of that which should be, and home shores?

        taking the moment
of vision in the flower, sex of the flower
posited among bees, the industry of honey, that *now*
broken again and again on those shores . . .

nothing but consciousness of consciousness
the decision of being exactly in the realm of light
that recitation of *here*

                    gone among the machines,
the singing machines grinding down,

                         and the ancients   with their ancient
songs.

lyrics for the bride of god

For N. & P.R.T.

SECTION: THE KITCHEN (5): THE COLLECTION

Prognostications   visions   omens   dreams
desires transformed into a telegram
it is time for her to come and collect her elected
she perishes of boredom in her own home
        and would devote some time to the home of the elected

which she'll paint, clean-out, spring-clean, fall-clean,
season-break
       until a temperate sun shines in always at the windows.

   And her eyes will not remember
      the crimes committed against her
        will not contain reproaches
         will not
           number the sins by the rings around the iris
   will not enumerate the trees of paradise

II

She'll take a hand of me for her purposes
and the other for his perhaps
and a leg of me for her walks along the ridges
and the other for his visitation to the hells
one side for the laying out of cities
the other for land-use and the fields
and in greater detail:
        the eye for seeing but of course
        and the nose for smell
        ears:hearing   /   mouth:taste
and the mind for the repartition of all things in their right places.

Of the other details we'll make
first a child in the mystery of her own belly
and the life which the child is to live for a long time
       and then attribute the power of surprising

to the ordinary, unadorned, untalented human body
so that a pair of eyes no very different from any other
will seem to one beholder like the very openings onto heaven
        I mean: we must enrich this world

        Though she come to take her own again
    is it not with the creation of the universe we are concerned
she and I in our   unfathomable love!

                            III

                    Parting the night like a forest
                    with that gesture of teaching
                    more beautiful than Justice
    we'll make of the way she came a broad swath cut through the forest
        and lie down inside it on the very divide
                Autumn will smell of Spring
            decay of birth   blood of the snow
        what there is in me to answer to my own
                ambitions rise from death
                            I have been wrapped in:

        and she will be a tree in my heart
                her roots pinning me down to this existence!

                            IV

Whether I see or not
                (according to the fancy of the wind
                the lateness of the heat
                the season's no to dying)
        all those great birds in line along the sky
                            sprung from her branches
                their shadow haunts the mind
                like wooden hawks above a chicken coop
                            and flesh or not

far kettles swirling with a thousand birds
invisible to all but angels now or not
yet I *have* seen them

and those wing-tips collecting me
scooping my eyes from their sockets

the flight midday perhaps if I can find the time . . .

SECTION: THE ARTEMISION (3)

Because there is a man waiting for you,
because there is a man waiting for you back in your loft,
because behind your life there is a shadow—
        though we run in step, though we walk
        exactly in step, and soon arm in arm, and soon
        body in body, and we say, almost at the same time
    WHAT IS THE MATTER WITH US
      IS THAT WE ARE FALLING IN LOVE WITH ONE ANOTHER
in the smooth stream of love, with the perfect unison of a forked twig,
toward the violets I didn't pick for you at dawn
        and which have aged by noon:

    O MAGIC EYE-OF-GOD FROM MEXICO
    your country given away to the weasels,
    your country transformed into dust . . .

but we are walking in circles round the house, wondering,
if that lunch took place, that lunch out of *La Bohème,*
during which our shoulders moved closer together
until at eve I put my arms under your breasts
and you leaned against me with your full weight,
and we are wondering
whether this is the time for our bodies to come together,
I am lying beside you on the bed, I think you came to fetch me,
there is a dowry of clothes between us, a snowfall of sheets
and you place your hands on your foundations
        as I attempt to touch them:

    You wonder about the bodies,
    about the fit of our bodies,
    and I wonder at my capacity,
    you are passive, your hound at your feet,
    you will not stroke your hound,
    you say you have not touched yourself: it does nothing for you,
    you must be woken from the snows.

We are bedded in the South, among the dews of blessings,
we have our male and female fears,
and we spend many hours talking, looking for recognition.

You have a back on you like a racing mare's
you have a front on you smells of mountain-lion,
you are afraid of your legs,
you fear your legs are too thick as they rise from thick feet,
but I say you begin like a tree rising solidly into this sky,
you rise from the bole of your tree into elegant branches,
your nipples: small berries in the mouth,

and it turns out you have your blood cupped in the moon,
cupped in the moon's month, Artemis,
and you are not sure whether I am a carnivorous hound or no.

It is four in the morning before the clothes are torn,
before the sheets are torn through and your blood flows on my tongue
as we grapple in a storm of agreement—
and it is four in the morning of May 25th, birth of our covenant,
it is four in the morning before our cry of recognition,
and at five we lie back with unearthly contentment
as light plays over branches and the exile is over.

SECTION: THE ARTEMISION (8)

This morning, at full tilt, a thrush slams to my window,
falls hurt to concrete and spins upon itself—
long streak of blood leaking from tongue in a drawn bow.
Bird finished says the mind. I've saved before,
                and will not leave to cat.
     Make night.
              Make night in box, place in dark room.
                     Pour brandy into beak to disinfect.
That way if he has to go he'll go in peace in darkness.
But he does not go. Three hours later, I free him to the trees.

And this same day you call me
with your voice of shadows,
you tell me the past goes out in front of you
               the shadow leaves
and the future enters at your back we don't yet know
but with a lovely confidence, as it was in your first courses
through the forests of youth with your puppies about you.
Bathing at the spring of the year, flesh white as dogwood,
your eyes white with the white of flowers,
                        we will finish at ease.

June 8th.
One lobotomized mongrel
shuts all the doors to peace.
This land, agrees a friend, is in the hands of curs,
this is no polity but a cheering squad
for a flag whose stripes bleed off it now, unquenchably.
             Make night. Take out the stars.
                 Make night: where do the bombs go over Hanoi,
                     over Haiphong, over the countryside:
do they all fall to the same crater,
that the country has failed so far to sink into the sea,
immemorial as Atlantis, a fragment in the imagination of Asia?

We are losing our pride,
poets of this Republic, while the bombs fall
and we discuss our salving metaphysics.
The possibility grows
that we will have to go out and get killed
against the tide of stupidity, worst of all human sins.
We are supposed to teach—take only that for one moment—
we are supposed to teach, say Blake, with the ONE IMAGINATION
and at the same time we are fed crass questionnaires daily
asking us to calculate the percentages of our time,
spent in the services of burrocrassy—
                              slice our imaginations,
divide them by twelve: apostles and Church,
whatever Church of Love is in our minds for this Republic.

The dogs of war are loose, Artemis.
More terrible than the dogs of hunting.
Their mouths slaver with blood, cur feeds on cur,
mindless, they rush through the streets of this uncaring township
that could be an h.q. for a Waffen S.S.,
they rush through the streets of the metropolis
choked in its doomsday ads and punctured lungs.
One lobotomized mongrel: king of the animals,
                    has closed the door to peace
                              /and dreams may suffer for the common cause.

What is the worth of a man
                    if he is downed like a bird by his fate
gunned down to silence in a pool of brains
                    his thoughts about him no longer usefulness
          gray mess for packs of rats and shareholders
                    stock-grubbers in the world he nearly owned,
he has now lost, and all his kindred,
                              to the tasteless rabble?

SECTION: THE INVISIBLE BRIDE (1)

"I have turned out the light
but it will not go dark . . ."

Once in my life, in her life,
Love looked at me a certain way with the look which doesn't lie
and I saw she'd been burnished to her ultimate beauty:
      I remember it was in the middle of something we were doing—
I looked up to say something light about some comment
      and for some reason / ah *what* reason on *that* night?
   THERE WAS THE LOOK OF FIRE
          as if she'd just achieved final illumination:
it was in the middle of something we were doing
            but the details escape me—

      Do not disturb this peace,
      darkness of the world,
      do not invade this house of bliss,
      this happiness wrested from the moment of life,
      do not disturb this hard-come-by,
      laboriously won victory over restlessness,
      don't rummage around in the furniture
      which has all become now one bed of peace:
          last manifesto of love,
     last chance on earth of this tradition:

and as I run out into the new, with eyes open into disaster,
          scream of man turned to deer
          boy to prey in the eagle's beak
          woman to laurel in the sun's embraces,
          that scream of longing satisfied /
          hiccup of satisfied desire / orgasmic cry
do not disturb this peace   for the fee my words shall pay you!

In her garret above the city, love lies a'dying
singing the arias she remembers one after another
waiting for her lover to show up
          so she can rise and feel

the scald of love in her bones
                    the green trees calling where they live
and, leaning on her elbow,
        she sings   she sings   she sings
            RINASCE!   RINASCE!   RINASCE!
(but is yet to perish),

From the century's lips my wife speaks out in her own name,
crying the lost man of her youth and all her gardens in disarray,
my children melt in the sun of another country
                    which is the country I have left
to come to this beginning of the deaths we have to die
        at the windows of this town
            bursting with cherry blossoms and chrysanthemums,
                suddenly/suddenly, in the middle of
in the middle of something we were doing,
the windows of the city full of petals and crying telephones!

They that have not learned the art of life
how shall they come to the art of *thanatos*
how start into the magnificent avenues of their dying,
opening out from the city into their childhood landscape,
and then, as shadows darken over eyes and ears,
begin into the alleys of death, turning aside from the highways,
wending their way from arteries into small veins,
dead-ends, cul de sacs, circular plazas,
where the dark rulers of the world sit on their golden stools,
drugs on their lips, pronouncing fates?

You are a region of my heart, death of the small entrances
    you are the population of that province
with big round eyes like an owl's, ringed with longing
                and you run toward empire
                as you would run to fat
                your population grows apace
                with a growl as of organs in churches
                a bellow of morning choirs:
                your population is growing
                        BEYOND ALL HEALTH

Cold has come over the city like a fang on the skin of revels
but the light is still the light of the Summer sky
                              in the days of our prosperity
—all of a sudden I see my children in the sky
                              laughing and dancing like children
in the middle of a very ordinary day
and I choke as if I'd tried to swallow a mountain
                    of loss and scandal
beyond the politics, beyond achievements,
the song in one's veins of careers and of renumerations,

AND AN ACID I CANNOT DILUTE EATS AWAY AT MY LIFE

I can hardly believe in human beings anymore
          I do not know how long I can maintain
     the credibility of life for myself
and then I remember the moment
     when Love looked at me a certain way and I hold,
               in the face of a greater light beyond naming,
and I do not sink, do not fall, do not cataract, do not ruin:
I DO NOT RUIN DOWN TOWARD ANOTHER WOMB TO BE REBORN
and I speak out at last with the voice which does not lie
at the depth where it becomes the voice of any man—

and I pay the price, Matron of the bright names of the Lord,
Angel of soaring birds, Queen of all that collects,
in the name of exile, selah, in the name of creation, amen:

to the rim where Love looked at me in a certain way
                              and never ceased from looking.

SECTION: THE INVISIBLE BRIDE (2)

> *"if one plate*
> *of the balance of the Law is destroyed*
> *what shall become of the other?"*

We sleep
        and beside us at the same height as our eyes
        the buzzards leave their tree and return to it
windmills of the dark sun
        turning over the brightness and the darkness
                    the mind's lobes
        now assenting, now saying no
the light and the dark like sails
                revolving in the mind

and sleep the only death we die and can awake from
    deep in the smell of our mouths
      our breath of meat and vegetation
    deep in the snore of our nostrils
            as if dragons curled in our furnaces,
                while I am busy dying
the voice awakes
    out of the day's decay

I journey to the terrible foundations,
    the spinal avenue,
      outside ethic, outside religion,
woman under and above / man secured in the middle—
           I am earthed at last, I am rooted—
yet as flesh falls away
    I am become as nothing in your pit of bone,
man withers and disappears
             woman shines like the grave—

The gates of the grave are below my house
guarded by the buzzard tree with its ferocious music,
nobody knows exactly where the descent begins,
where the pilgrims go down to the shadows of unremunerative death:

but it is hereabouts—and perhaps it is under your body
                    perhaps your great length hides it—
who knows whether your stride does not cover the pit
        as you walk in the dark air of my dreams
                and whether I do not begin this journey again in your embraces:

and it is a journey of birth make no mistake,
                        though scandal and terror attend it,
        for all the sweet souls singing friendship around us,
I am manifestly that sower of pain I never thought to be:
        I don't glory in the role, very far from it,
but as the leaves fall in the hard rain
                        in the never-ending Autumn of this life,
carajo courage claws at my loins and rakes them
                        inside the pit of carnage.

I would like to leave this house and go out into poverty
I would like to let the buzzards move over to a tree
exactly above the house and drown it in a white rain of loss
        I would leave these birds to their end
                        and enter the embrace of the eagle
                        burning in the midday sky
                        consumed in a great dream of desire
        and pass my heart through my mouth to his beak
                        leaving my body on the dole of waters.

            The children present themselves in the far distance
                    at the pillars of the grave in your sex
                the children at the gate cry and sing out
                        in the piping song of their loss
                we have no father   /   we have no father
                    BUT AH MY POOR MASKS
                            your father
                        fatherless himself
                        motherless himself

(Adjustment   *(One child smiling*
of clothing before   *not quite certain*
coming toward him)   *if the parent will*
(Glance to see if   *listen or not/ indeed*
noticed)   *if it is he or not)*

YOUR FATHER HAS GONE OUT INTO THE STARS
HE HAS GONE OUT TO WHERE IT IS NOT POSSIBLE

                              TO HAVE CHILDREN ANYMORE

                                        save only words

I had not thought to cause such devastation
                    and the secret of the fall around me
is that I require the excitement of carnage
            for the work I am perpetually about to do:
It would appear that I cannot move
                    without inflicting suffering on those I love
I waste away in my poverty surrounded with words
I hear the words I utter preparing the Spring
                    in the dying trees around the house.

We go out into the stars
leaving a sad cortege of mourners for our lives,
the children wheel overhead with the black birds of consumption
pointing beak downward at the gates of the infernal regions,
the doors in the birds' wings turn over and over in their dreams,
under their eyelids cities fall and countrysides are devastated,
the little roots play among the entrances to the hells
   grubbing among death's foundations
                    with the still small voices of new life.

SECTION: THE INVISIBLE BRIDE (6)

"O Queen Injustice
how widespread is thy kingdom,
give us this day our daily loss
our daily waste
our daily excrement . . ."

Have been in orbit so long
  can hardly quit it
      the deathly silence
          read as hope or despair:
cannot tell any longer /
             nothing continues to happen
     cruciform tablet
  dark with a thousand could-bes
   one or two meaningless words from time to time
  and space to space
   crossing the oceans as I had prophesied—
  from shore to shore
shade of the shade of absence
             not going dark
        trying to make it / out of this destiny,
    a weakness in the eyes
          preventing it . . .

I think I move quickly: I move slowly,
I sit and stare,
    there is nothing I want to do more than to stare
at anything that falls under my eyes.
    I do move slowly, like an old man,
          and put down my foot slowly,
and stutter when I speak to certain people
       (those who are close to her theme)
and cannot remain alone
  for fear of becoming two, not one,
    (and have been taken away   days I cannot remember)
for fear of becoming multitude
of people I don't know walking around the house

and talking in louder voices
than I can handle.
                I have walked head on into a locomotive,
                it has flattened me against the wall.

The night is exceedingly long,
                the day most short,
the night very short, the day:
"a century is but a moment in Her sight."
I am trying to understand the people passing through this room
when there is no one in the room except she and I talking
           talking
                talking do you realize
                      we've been talking
some thirty-six hours without cease?
                That skull, for instance,
owned a long time: the face cosmeticized,
    trepanation, five minutes go by,
as I break from speech with her, stare at the skull,
and say, after the longest while I needn't feel apologetic for,
do you realize we are alive and he has been dead here so long?
        and she says: did you never know him before?

Which is the way people pass, in and out of us,
as if we were laid flat and they were layers of us,
    but from another time, almost as if
      they were fragments of a family forgotten,
a family misplaced long ago, buried by one who had to return
    many lives later to the same place, to disinter them.
      She who throws herself out of windows,
        in the gyres of her morning flights,
    is happy with them also.
But I do not want to see anyone I have known in this life,
my heart thumps like a cold engine started up too fast
at the thought that I would have to open the door to someone I know:
to her shadow in flight   /   as she'd come in
                  to batter me down,
    and look I said to her,
I wouldn't really *recognize*—and the scenario would be:
(yes she said, yes she said quickly, of course, I understand)

There are different sorts of people she said
     some are angels—
             and pass through
  not supposed to be stopped
     on their way to somewhere I suppose,
O so beautiful   /   so loving
  they make a lot of questions for oneself
they make one ask and ask
         // but in a comfortable way //
     you know?
and: what if all these people you see were but the screens
     —several beauty—
of one whose inner heart
     wanders forever over the earth and cannot rest
     asking nothing more but to fall
down through forgetfulness
        to some new, unified beginning?

SECTION: AMERICA (2): SEEN AS A BIRD

The light in the skull of the bird
       tugging her down
              she'll fly by the rest of her life,
mirror of sky among leaves,
           in low grasses at morning,
                 mirror of high sky in low and of heaven in high
                     along the milky way—
her eye—the order of the heavens
       falling   /   falling with the weight of damp stars
               down flocks of other birds
               down through t.v. antennae
                       funnel of space
             above the house at last
                 great fields of light above her
         over Cape May

Birds in layers on the sky
a flock of certain birds above a flock of others and besides
         yet a third flock
         kettle of broadwing on the spiral air
            cut to the quick by geese along the shore
                 and here the blackbirds scatter like ink-shot—
the sky has great depth
         the depth opens on without end higher and higher

        Alighieri describing the major angels as birds of God:

        Take here the little birds for the kingdom of heaven,
         the little birds for the banners of God—
and say what we love about them is simply the system:
that they are all of one set, yet different colored,
         id est—diversity within unity, heraldic counterpoint
         of certain colors where others are expected to be
—my dream as a child, the interchange of colors—
         what gives my mind peace, my mind peace, my mind peace

immense fields of light traversed by angels

/ / /   over Cape May . . .

II

Seeing her as a bird,
               looking within that mind
for the cut of our sparks in each mirror shard,
her flight breaks over and over
                   as she tumbles down
     through cloud, through stricken dawn-dark, and bait and lure,
                                        TO
     if she be (for example) that one-eyed falcon, sparrow-hawk,
        bird of the year,
                 so must in nest have lost
       one half of strike-force within the head
yet falls on sodden sparrow in his trap
       waiting for tear of talons and her take
                       his cheep toward
                       his and her father both.

We'll have, above all, her movement
              and her descent, layer on layer,
                   through the bright cloud of our blood
and the exact description of her rapine
          when she comes to fetch us
            fingernail by fingernail

       I mean   of course   talon.

     Look long ago the sky had many birds
     look long ago the sky had many colors
       and now we have the chicken only
       and the sparrow like an aerial rat.
We mourn like antiquarians for the world's colors
     while the rest of the world makes do.

And she is bird, falling,
      and I am bird, passing from behind that branch
to this branch in front of your eyes, and you are bird,
      hopping to middle branches in a three-tiered forest
and he is bird flits to the first branch in the foreground of /
        your alien life under heaven-home:

     and they all mirror each other, looking with bright eye
     periscope to the shard of the inner mind,
     at the tone of your color today bright cousin,
     and the shade of your tint tomorrow, bright female cousin—
     and, *by God,* I think they talk, Alice would say that morning
     as she broiled the two budgerigars side by side on a spit,

     while the white heart of the sky, ignorant of all color
           arched over, archangelical
           throbs in restricted place
       the pure white heart of the sky, ignorant of all color
           with rims of morning

        Elanus leucurus, minute particular,
        Coyote Hills, on San Francisco Bay,
        November seven-one ("great bird of God")

           goes into somersault
          revised and held thereafter
         and, looking down—
                    buckle of elbow forward
                  drag back of pinions in the wind
                  slow crash at twilight angles—

(the planes in circles overhead, ever diminishing)

     slow fall to grasses like the dying snow.

SECTION: AMERICA (11): AT GLOUCESTER, MASS., AFTER FOREIGN TRAVEL

At Gloucester, Mass., after foreign travel,
   Labor Day mists
        the lovely breath of one more Summer dying out,
the sea
      swelled contrapuntally as we swam
and a smell of old furniture came up from the water
                into the dusting sunlight . . .

As if all the woods that had gone down into the sea
              surfaced to farewell Summer
the boats crossed and crisscrossed over the drowned
             and the great feast of work
crimson with lobster shells, stubbed toes and girls' bandannas
             set round the pink of nipples
in loose red shirts   /   O flag of love over America the damned!

We went down to the sea
all the poets together
and gave ourselves up to the waters
              in various positions of loss:
I realized that I had never died into water
           and within five minutes
after giving myself completely to the wave

              I did about ten things
never done in my life before
such as: throwing my body like a javelin into the waves
spreading myself like a banner on the swell
somersaulting in the deep
holding the sand's thighs in my hands
             and all the fear was gone —

We had spent the whole day looking for loons and grasses
old Dogtown had risen for us from the ground
and Charles Olson's floor and windowboards full of dates
had defied the policy on National Monuments —

white building slats among the red stripes
                    the stars on my Union Jack
exclusive to the night:

                    and she seen rightly
had no need to be touched
                    she seen rightly
became a thousand faces one after another
                    seen rightly
there was no face the world could take on which was not her face
                    and a golden aura

red with cheap scents raved around her hair.
                    Oh the hands that went out,
the bodies that moved out toward her on our belief,
                    Labor Day, Gloucester, Mass.,
the copulations that sped toward her on the arrow of sight
                    drawing no flesh at all
out of its sheathing!

                    The America he dreamed never existed.
                    cause of lost causes—
                    but dreamed it with the throat of need
                    the passionate thirst of a tramp
                    sweat on his whiskers.
                    And she in whose hands lies my life
                    brings her creased eyes to town

brings her body like a banner
she said she could not use
  advertising ships, and land, and whispers among hutments,
and "today," he said, "today,"
        "tears of blood coming out of the ground
at what has become of this Republic
                    which was to be the laughter of the world!"

If it be true   /   that this polity
has killed Allende for instance   /   has killed Neruda
if it be true that Spain is being repeated—billed to this polity—
                    then the devices of the world of ice

the hanging in the maws of the old windmill the great Giver devised
shall be but childplay to what awaits
our shabby emperor in his greasy feathers /-/-/-

encore une fois l'refrain

Swallow on the air

mackerel on the sky
mackerel in the water
swallows on the sea

stitching silver to silver

in the heart's water:

I am so glad to be home!

I have laid up a world of words
for the immortal gods of this Republic
that all the 50 stars might sing in unison together!
Our moods of love
as they will seize and shake us all our lives:
wood rising from the sea, trees soaring on first shores,

the Adam-hut, its ghost,

I am so glad to be home!

SECTION: LA TRAVIATA (4): WOMAN'S EXPENSIVE, ART'S PRICES FOLLOW

Alexandre Dumas Fils to Sarah Bernhardt:
"My Dear Sarah,
Allow me to offer you a copy of "*La Dame aux Camélias*"
                              which has become rare.
What makes this copy unique is the *als.* you will find
                              inserted at the 212th page
which is very close to the letter in the printed text at that point.
                    This letter was written
by the real Armand Duval some forty years ago
                              : it doesn't make him any younger.
His age was your own son's today.
                    The letter turns out to be
THE ONLY PALPABLE THING to have survived that story.
                    You own it as of right
since it is you who have just resurrected the dead past.
                    Keep it in any case
as a souvenir of the lovely evening, last saturday
                    and as an unworthy keepsake
of my very great admiration and warmest gratitude.
                                        With this,
I applaud you with all my strength and embrace you
                    with all my heart. A.D. 1/28/1884"

Alexandre Dumas Fils to Marie Duplessis:
"My Dear Marie,
I am not rich enough to love you as I would wish,
nor poor enough to be loved as YOU would desire it.
                    Let's both of us forget:
a name which must, by now, be quite indifferent to you,
a happiness for me become impossible.
                    No use telling you my sadness,
since you already know how much I love you.
                    Farewell.
You have too much heart to misunderstand the causes of my letter,
too great a mind not to forgive it me. A thousand memories.
                         A.D. 8/30/1845."

Marguerite Gautier to Armand Duval:
"When you will read this note, Armand, I will already be
another's mistress. We're through.
Go back to your father my friend, *dite a la giovine, si bella e pura,*
—your sister chaste, our misery unknown—
at whose side you will soon forget what this lost Marguerite
you loved a moment will have made you suffer,
who owes you the few happy moments of a life she hopes ends soon.
                                                        Marguerite Gautier."

To Marie Duplessis, alias Marguerite Gautier, alias Violetta Valéry:
"Madam:
        Anxious to redeem an adolescence distinguished by no romantic adven-
tures, I beg the honor to be received into your bed—there to enjoy the favors
so inordinately praised by those fortunate enough to have been your contem-
poraries. It is said of you, despite the great care you have of adorning your
beauty, and of administering to it with all the resources at your lovers' com-
mands, that you are a woman of heart and wit, rather than a plaything of
riches. I am a poet, born of the underworld, now come to rest in a small corner
of Pennsylvania in the United States. My youth was spent in dreams of un-
achievable love. Above all, I have always regretted not being born in the time of
phaetons and silver clouds, white picnics in cool parks, and all the refinements
of music and dance I associate with the waltz. It is not so much that I have been
unloved by women—or even that I have not enjoyed the favors of a great cour-
tesan—but rather that, like men of my temperament born under any clime, I
have rarely exhausted my passions in the one and only, but have always run
after the many in a desperate attempt to make time stop.

        O Violetta, Marguerite, Marie, Alphonsine,
                                by whatever name they call you,
I learn that, when Alexandre met you in his troubled search,
the camellia you wore at your breast was still tinged with red.
Wherefore you told him to return when it would have faded—
or, in my reading, when it would have become again white.
Know of my intimacy that I am so kindred to the blood of woman
that the great meetings of my life have taken place under its sign.
Welcome me back then, to where there are no fathers and mothers,
take me to the altar of your body in the keep of perfect time,
and, since you cannot hack the scent of any other flower, believe me
        Always yours in a perfumeless time. Nathaniel Tarn. 6/9/1973."

100

SECTION: LA TRAVIATA (11): THE LAST ILLUSION

(When I had parted from her who'd held me seven years)

to the land at the other end of the wind,
lovely island through the world's age
shaped like a whale in the wine-blue ocean,
beyond the sunken precinct where philosophers had ruled,
the singing shrine where no sorrows reign,
where the roses are like weeds in the streets of town,
where no punishing storm, no snow, and never rain
foil tools at work in fields, while men bask under trees,
and corn's self-sowing and self-harvested

      (not tenderness for sons, duty to age,
      nor love I owed to wife that should have gladdened her)

to the land whose rivers may well have led to Eden,
the first sin skirted on the shoals,
which is nothing but the name the past gives to the future,
the first, or apple, sin: *o felix culpa!*
the second sin of corn: *o felix culpa secunda!*
sailing for wisdom with compass and canvas
beyond the borders of the inhabited world
to a place where there is a denudation of people,
where the birds talk like scholars in many languages

      (my men being slow and old when we came to that gate
      chose to deny the world in the sun's track
      and with our stern turned toward morning . . .)

but the island was peopled with playful children
believing paper spoke and asking beads from the sky,
begging for colors from the sky in trade for corn,
that were too cheap in the salons of turquoise —
and we were those who had come from under the world
to take their own world from them.
Quicquid praeter Africam, et Europam est, Asia est:
Was *this* Cathay? — these were not wise enough to be souled . . .

And it came to me in a dream, when I was grappled by them,
that I was brought before a splendor of feathers
and ordered to lay my head down on a stone,
but the child came from behind him, taking my head in her arms,
asking my life. Whereat, she was given it
and I made a son to the King. Being later told
this was a simile of entrance into kingship, no genuine danger—
but took it out a little on my reading public

and also that the land at the other end of the wind
was full of nubile beauties who sang and danced for men,
after which they took us into their house
and everyone wanted me, crying "Love me, love me,"
so that it seemed I could not have endured so many loves /
but this was not prostitution as it turned out,
nor even free love, nor the beginning of commune,
but merely the offering of a companion, for a luxury at night.

II

She had argued that she would give up her wealth and follow me that was
now the one man on earth she could abide. As she said this, her black hair
glistened as if moist with mist, or it could have been tears from her native
sky. She confessed she had been born on the great island at the end of the
world, and that it was time she returned there in any event to savior the
natives. For she had adopted an orphan child by mail the month before.
She spoke of her youth as half a horse, when she raced the clouds in the
southern deserts, and of her battling with waves as tall as towers under the
spruces of her birthright. Whence from half snake, she had gone to fish,
and finally bird, in other realms of North and West. She possessed the
land, *dueña* thereof. And was ready to purchase many acres more, on our
two accounts.

But had not reckoned with the languor
that had crept into her bones in the ancient world
where she sat for years oblivious to the people
in blaze of music. She had become addicted
to the culture of the terminal empires, denying
and neglecting the simple crafts of her own yard.

It was opera for her every night, fine meals,
camellias every morning, and pearls,
it was the company of fine gentlemen, who, more or less discreetly,
kept her in the style to which she had become accustomed.

And when she had attempted to turn toward what she thought was
"home," maps and charts had powdered in her hands—and had we
followed her directions, we would have lost ship and crew both in great
batter of rock. When the oldest woman of Europe landed on her native
shore, many dusky maidens came to her crying, and holding her shoul-
ders, whose names were Pocahontas, and Malitzin, and Tekakwitha, and
Sacajawea, and Jacataqua, lamenting: "Now that thou art come, María
Colomba, daughter of doves, must we lie down and be reduced to dust?"
But she undressed herself of her crinolines, and appeared in the perfec-
tion of her own darkness, and ordered them that they should denude
themselves likewise down to their very own silks, and follow her in the
dance. Whereupon the scenario was enacted as aforesaid—but here, I
enjoyed them all one after another ... Only, when I awoke in the morning,
it was as if fallen from a great height, from an ocean cliff, and there was not
one companion of them all to bind my wounds and comfort.

III

And I am become as a land of ghosts

as a tree full of bird song but no birds

where the mist clings to branches like cotton

and the wind drawls mourning

From the other side, it was as if we had been calling for this, as if the
weight of our need were such that it had magnetized the seas, and called a
great pole to ourselves up from the place where the sun sets, and which we
had named: the western gate,

and had placed all our dreams there, in who knows what hands ...

and as if all the singers had assembled on the old land's shores, standing before the flattened doors and tables at the cliffs' edge that had seemed to be made as springboards for the great passage, and with but a short elegy for those they were to leave behind—who had lost the sense of hearing— they all, with a common accord in history, leapt into the westering sea, and were carried by fish or whale or albatross to the ocean's furthest edges . . .

there, with darker women than themselves, to make new races . . .

but, having carried choice gifts to the land's King, who, though he did not at first condescend to like them, became at last so enamored of possessions that he turned all the energies of his people to their fabrication, and made slaves of them until they also wanted nothing but these goods, and, at last, the whole land having been delivered into the hands of those whose chief business was to make, advertise, barter and sell these goods, at whatever price, at whatever sacrifice and whatever beastliness in the reduction of men to animals of burden, who were no longer THE PEOPLE:

so that the ghosts at last, even they, had lost their tongues . . .

then it seemed indeed that we HAD come from under the world

to take their own world from them . . .

IV

The last woman of the old dispensation has gone back to her dust.
And the first woman of the new world is going back to her dust.
She keeps on changing the color of her hair, as in a movie,
she becomes a blonde on the way to Kalifornia, West of the West,
she is an androgyne going out into Space, which is West of Kalifornia,
lugubrious in a night of spiders, they all leave for distant lots.

And when the people of this continent have made their shopping list:
the oil of the other people of the world and their labor,
their blood . . . . and their labor, their flesh . . . . and their labor,
they then fall to buying health and happiness and parity freedoms,

then they think of purchasing a second automobile and two frigidaires
and three sets of air-conditioning devices and a radio-clock-t.v.

and all that done, they come to the places they have baptized
with all the variants of the word *Hope*, which means hope for bargains:
Hope-Well, and Hope-Truly, and New Hope, and Good, Clean, Used-Hope,
 and, leaving behind any reality whatsoever,
  they buy the shoddy, the useless, the ugly and the bad
in the name of the singers of liberty who left our world so long ago.
At night, when everyone is drunk, they piss on the town's trees,
shit in the streets, and masturbate in the parking lots

and then gang-bugger the injun princess in the municipal square

where they had left her only some years back

 as she bounced out of the forest:

 infin che'l mar fu sopra noi richiuso . . .

the house of leaves

"To Everybody"
—ANDREA TARN, 1776

WIND RIVER BALLAD

Wind River O Wind River
tonight I go to my Bride
Wind River O Wind River
tonight she lies by my side
and all your mountains and all your lakes
and all your bushes and trees
will sound like silence to the noise she makes
with her innumerable bees

Wind River O Wind River
tonight I taste of her breast
Wind River O Wind River
her milk is the milk of the blest
and all your flowers and all your leaves
and all your cattle and sheep
won't match the riches that she receives
when for love she has made me weep

Wind River O Wind River
tonight I pray to my stars
Wind River O Wind River
she'll heal every one of my scars
and all your people and all your ghosts
and all the groans of the slain
won't match the face of her heavenly hosts
or the print of her love on my brain

THOSE IN WASHINGTON

For Roberto Sanesi

Out breakfastless, at dawn, for warblers
  Virtue
            of
                    solitude
               acute perfume:
      pines and anticipation!

Spring come around again — familiar
                       resurrection.
Scatter of music.
The tanager flames from his tree-top
              the grosbeak weeps with his breast
victory fires.

                 And from tree to tree
quick as needles
         almost invisible
     the little people / pygmies / the jewels
       of the world of air.

American Redstart dressed in fire and mourning
     cool, elegant, the Black and White
     in stripes and spats,
perhaps the Blackthroateds, but not certain,
     one with a back of sky
I've chased so long and never found —

          so high
       so high in the trees
    it is as if the wind had cried
       his words had   settled there
   still beating like hearts in the branches

and violence of song!
   destruction of all we build
   in that many-throated passion!
  the towers tumbled   /   walls
                              fallen to rubble in that song!

her hair
   woven with wings as with jewels
              a radiance in her eyes as of bright feathers
                  in the quiet wood
   her body
              a tunnel in which the jewels leap like flames
                        along the trees of its sides
           through which I go   deaf to all but the music
                              and those falling cities

                        I no longer desire . . .

SIN ALTERNATIVA

For George Buchanan

I am so thick that this world's problems,
the material problems refuse to go through me,
stick to my hands like flies to walls,
like men white as the walls with hunger
and my skin also they refuse to leave
buzzing close to the skin longer than you would ever
believe they could endure the swatting.

I am beginning to understand how it is possible
for people in the very prime of age
to look forward to a long
uninterrupted sleep. Day wears from morning
until evening, down, and you fall
gratefully into the arms of your bed
and if there is someone in them you hardly notice.

Those who are weavers of light
cling tenaciously to this world and allow
the light to come through their skins in such a way
that only the moral problems wear them down.
But these bring also the ever-restless guilts.
You would think that the vulture eventually
might finish his piece of liver
or that the rat would come to an end of gnawing
his sliver of intestine.
Nor does this happen either.

For those who continue to wish to work down here,
life has to provide some means of ending.
It switches the powers off one by one:
our needs, the joy one takes in them.
Eventually most of the things that have pleasured us
are wearied by rubbing away
or deadness of desire in the marrow.

Then we lie down and prepare ourselves
to be transformed entirely into light
in order that we might be devoured by no other life.

OLVIDO INOLVIDABLE

For Octavio Paz

The suns of all the galaxies shine suddenly together
the world's blood unfreezes and
runs through the forest of our veins,
we go with dream-ease through all our recognitions:
she had looked for me a long time between the snows
with the darts of the Arrow-Bearer,
I have drunk of her blood at the source
and eaten of her amber load
and washed in the scald of her tears,
she is someone you know and have not seen for a while
you will see her again soon
because her time is wedding to my time
and we move everywhere in step together,
she makes gold in the daytime
and at night she mints silver
under her feet as she comes the dawn grasses grow,
she draws the great bow of our life
the arrow flies straight for the mark and hits heart,
she has found me again after much travail,
the forest is open again, the deer leap,
the hounds belt baying like mad water,
sun and moon wake in each other's arms surprised
and the stars make music together incessantly.

AFTER JOUVE

For Henri & Nô Seigle

Think a little of the sun in your youth
The sun which shone when you were ten years old
Surprise do you remember the sun in your youth
If you focus your eyes well
Watch narrowly
You can still catch a glimpse of it
It was pink
It took up half the sky
You could look at it straight in the face you could
Surprise but it was so straightforward
It had color
A dance it had desire
A heat
An extraordinary ease
It loved you
All that in the middle of your age sometimes
        running on rails along the morning's forests
You thought you imagined
Deep in yourself
It's in the heart that the old suns are put away
It has not moved there is that sun
Of course yes there it is
I have lived I have ruled
I illuminated with such a great sun
Alas it's dead
Alas it has never
Been
Oh that sun you say
And yet your youth was unhappy

::

There's no need to be king of Jerusalem
Every life questions itself
        Every life asks itself

And every life waits
Every man travels the same way everything is limited
    how to see more
And we went and invented ourselves machines
They came smashing everything drilling the old earth
    filling the old air
Waves rays shining axes
And there you are my power has grown terrible
My anxiety also
My instability
I can't sit still any more
I search I become
I'm no longer my real age I toy with everything
But my God hoary war has come back and scarcely changed
Human blood has only one way of flowing
Death has only one way of flowing
Death has only one step always the same to fall upon me
Space has shrunk my soul it is newer
I do not say better
I would not dare

::

We are far from stewing in resignation but
Our pleasure is always the guiltiest
For if grief should need justification grief is the earth
    our city grows on
Joy purity
Don't come near
It's in relation to our joy
That our vanity seems so pitiful
We're in such a rush
Our doubts are so old
Yes it's with our joy that we tremble
Degenerate child
Yet the spirit suspended over universal sorrow
Said you have senses make them give back your pleasure
And that is bitter
More bitter

And that speeds up somehow in bitterness
For us

::

Eternal Judge
What power stupidity has the stars shine for stupidity
Light suits it so well the great trains take it everywhere
Every town is its meeting place its pleasure park
And on sundays one catches sight of its family picnic
What glory after the war
For disorder and lightheartedness
Everyone lives so much better
What an achievement for the boxer
The poet
Still lives on the fifth floor ailing of an old hunger
Meditates on his approaching death looking to be eternal
No don't think he loves death as he used to love it
He asks questions
He tries groping
He sighs he is delirious
And life he thinks would be really marvelous if

::

The greatest business is dying and we don't know a jot of it
Those who came by don't come again
But I must admit that I'm not anxious
I no longer believe in them now
Without understanding I wipe them out they are dead
Of silence
Complicity
Perhaps it isn't a business after all perhaps death is
    nothing to us
Or yet again perhaps
Everything is for this only death this great gateway
    this favored haven
Where the ship comes home
But no for I don't believe in happiness and I don't
    believe in death

I must tell you that I am ultimately certain of being immortal
Essential vanity

::

When young I loved time
I couldn't stand being the youngest
I loved the grass when it seeded the trees
    when they spread themselves like music
I loved the old
Now I shadow the other side of the hill
The downward slope
I no longer know I've tasted many eras
Calm will come perhaps with age

::

How much contempt man has for this mouth he adores
But he's found extasy there he goes on running after extasy
Vitality
He goes on demanding the smell taste and color of
    women's bodies
Their elasticity
Their lie
Whatever in the mother-of-pearl flesh smiles chastely
    at death
And then after that
His sadness comes
Which he recognizes

::

How hard we've searched—miracles we are miracles
Nothing
This world was straight infinite now it is curved
    slipping one into the other
Man's vision has grown but it is backed by less and less
Thought is thin feeble useless a trail of mist like the Milky Way
    like the Milky Way

While the world is matter is spread out is terrifying
    is real like the wall of hell
Thought smiles because it is going to die it could be

::

These opposing stars
One which lit the fire and one which was lit by the fire
He who gave and she who asked action and mystery
He who throws and she who gestates are always present
    at whatever moment
Herald and Hunted swirl in the blue egg of space he and she
Then reunited
They make up a long song with heights and depths
Always falls always springs
They go back as they had come
Always the wave-shaped curve the heights the depths
There that's all
And the sea's hem the leaves thrust the terrestrial fanfare
    of mountains
Don't be afraid of your sadness it is mine
It is ours it is his his it is hers
Oh grandeur
Be not afraid here is peace life life is admirable
Life is vain
Life is admirable life is admirable it is vain

FROM: THE FIRE POEM

2.

Immortally beautiful
    as she passed
that day in the flame of her hair
    with the fast eyes of ships,
stopped Rome that day, stopped Athens,
    stopped, even, Jerusalem,
stopped woman's city whole
        and FLARED
like a new culture
  sail of her being   /   over the rooftops
like a great pilgrimage
  the birds, the animals, the grasses
        of the city
  saying (in new found voices)
this newfoundland:
look / she is going / in that flame of hair
     toward a furnace,
toward a revolution
     —immortal beauty—
there is no news of yet
             in all these voices—
but news there will be. Soon. Soon.
          After the night.

4.

Nothing but the night, frankly,
  nothing, no nothing but the night—
as I have said many a time
  noche oscura del alma / *y de la civilización*
and then
  under the brink of a black hat

(felt, gypsy-like)
    the red face of the goddess
                      androgynous a little
breathing familiar fire over my tongue,
pouring the wine into my throat,
the molten gold
    a day of happiness distills—
the eyes like witch's eyes,
    like two live coals
from her leather country,
    the teeth like children's bones
or the bones of birds—white, white
                  and the smile sailing,
surf on an unknown sea with a dawn rim
                  on the day of discovery.

7.

To be happy like this day
    many days need to have been lived,
much coal needs to have been fired,
many beings to have informed that coal,
many fates to have woven those beings—
    to be rich like today
    with her stillness beside me
like a pulse in the blood, that homely a matter,
    yet how miraculous—
to have eaten as we ate today
    like kings at table,
and to have spent
    like princes lavishly comparing
the goodness of each earth the gods had gifted them—
    to be at peace now:
with the energy burnt
    and not in vain,
breeding, out of its ashes, energy again,
        many fires must have been set
        under the phoenix,
        much wood cut down

to build the pyre,
many great deeds performed by us together
and many gifts of each one's life
to beast or conqueror,
        or to each other,
in a past almost too distant
to bear the knowledge of
        with equanimity.

8.

How can,
    how CAN that noise,
that noise of fire, or noise of powered waters
    come from (from nothing) and from
so much silence?
Was poor   Was starving   The dead had said
    "We have seen you too often."
And I had told them
    "Will pay you one more ransom" —
always one ransom,
each time more blood, more time, more blighted life.
Until I was afraid
I would not have enough
        —nor would there be enough
in the whole city—
    to ransom that dead one again,
to bring her up, silent and all-forgiving,
    like the sun from under the sea
by the stream's side
    back to snake's meadow.
The payment fell into the void, I weary.

And she rose up beside me as if the mist were praying.

9.

I would have the stars
        bow down to her,
I would have the days
        take on her name
and be her namesakes,
        I would have the moon
sail through the sky for her smile
        and hers alone,
having no other motion
        than in her pleasure,
I would have my words
        live and die on her lips
with no other function
        than to give her voice,
call her one day,
        saying "I've finished,
we can go up to the great sky,
might as well start to name
        the land from there."
I would simplify the word
        until she stood inside it,
the word incarnate,
        the only goddess.

FROM: BETWEEN DELAWARE AND HUDSON

For Robert Kelly

2. First Movement on the Delaware

Her right foot lifts the wind
as she leans upon it
      it presses into earth,
we go to bird together,
      she-falcon at my wrist,
below the revolutionary tower.

Under her wings as she flies
from my right wrist, the avenues of air
open to talon-tread
      and she has risen
height of knee relaxing and unfolding
      into a flower of movement.

Streaking in liberation
across the wide divide—
      the space between her talons—
in wing-pits leaves unfurl,
the trees come to conclusions
      renting the light.

Moves the other foot sideways
putting down without weight
begins to shift the body to the lure
      of the next moment:

trap of the whole migration
her wingspread holds the birds,
they name their names in distant trees,
      the stream sings underneath.

and her hands, loose at the wrists,
taking their stance from mine

float up into the wind her feathers make
        far ahead of her sight,

she draws in wings,
plummets to treetop, pinions bend
all summer in her taut embrace,
        bow of the mountains:

        Where is the arrow
as her hand falls through air
fingers trailing like feathers
or tails of butterflies—
colors like streams
        within the light?

In turn of time, in keeping,
tells me the names of all my battles.
Her hands have come to rest across my hands:
we prepare the next position.

4. Blithewood on Hudson

Since he had said: let there be a poem,
(whose wide arms encompass the gate
        and whose world-body,
I suddenly remember,
belongs to the order that might be hers)
        let it be so:

in the octagonal room,
her washing done, she takes my starved
and therefore clumsy body into hers,
breaking the rim of habit—and I scream
with all the ghosts in the house,
running my fingers down
        her night-dew,

shudder again under her sleep . . .

Morning. The lawnmowers
power the gardens, the roses hum
that are stars somewhere in her keeping
and not yet out / the southern birds
mad with the north, careen around
daughters of Hudson sunning their backs,
formal gardens, fathomless lawns.

We wander through my fatherhood of her,
everywhere she is taken for my daughter
that will not bond with birds,
that will not wing me from moment to moment
and recognize, so that I may remember
and heat in the gloom like a kiln
on our return,

shudder again under her waking . . .

And cannot marry her in any sense,
cannot assume her skin
under my hands,
Delaware, Delaware of the golden back:
father of wolfbane and mandrake,
she circumscribes my palsy.

        Letting it be so:
the rooms are empty in the morning
and the memories empty.
I stifle under her sleep, wake and get up
walk out beyond the city's curve

    never more to see her in this life.

5. Second Movement, on the Delaware

She turns to the right
        bringing the bud of air
to easy flowering,
leans forward on the right, as if to fly,

the left heel lifts:
she is so vulnerable

and saw her as a child
     for the first time
who had been such a woman to me,
     muse in starlight,
her nose in my affairs
up to the hilt,

saying: "look at my beauty, my beauty,
the beauty I see in my hunger for this world" —
     but could see
only her own beauty, and not another's
only her hunger /
          protecting those wild foods.

Then: the internal wings
that speak to each other of great goodness given
mentioned that out of the mouths of sucklings
—even she who had sucked at this manhood—
the path of their own stars and the era's stars
conjunct in time: out of the mouths
     our ends would come
unlooked for.

And we run, we dance, we fly around her
who are looking for the motionless wisdom
until her stillness gains us
  and move and stillness both
lapse into happiness.
     She lifts the left foot

extends it before her, the body gliding
to face the future fully
and she troubles us with a growth of wings,
an understanding around the head like an aura,
speaking to us in the tongues of silence,
the silence responding in our skulls,
with the words we would know
     if we but voiced them . . .

Rise of the Spirit of Independence:
the tower this morning is weary,
the trees are full of bird noise
   but no birds.

I shall continue to prove us.

8. Movement Itself

Kinesis—
   movement,
the pest
   keeping us in action,
forcing us
   beyond the momentary desire
into the invisible curve of our lives /
yet knowledge beyond that moment
   not clear in any reasoning
(any more than the movement of armies
   to define a state),
but in *collegium*, the total mind, o.k.

And the plunge of wings
   the guiding archangels
     of this era,
working (and with their immobilities)
   for the clarity of the state—
her voice droning away in the background
   among the voices of warblers,
her profile (eyes and nose covered with feathers)
   becoming brighter
as the tower rises above the hill,
carries each scale of its body
   into the light.

Kinesis
  of the holy stars across the firmament,
the movement of the profile
   turning, with no thought for the past,

her voice comes out of me with no bidding,
        my mouth as if between her thighs,
            —the bearded woman,
the breasted man, exploding cunt-cock—
    giving birth to the tower,

Working in another time
not in accordance with the time I'm given
        which is another's
and a prison /
                I abdicate
to work in my own time
        like a bird flying—
the provision of food
        in the world's hands:
swallows on the Delaware bridge
        launched at the wind
and back to the bridge with their prey.

That my voice is not my own any more
has been becoming clear to me for some time:
it comes out of, mark, out of
I know not what mouth, mouths, paramouths,
other entrance, door, gate or passage (of any sort)
            vulva or womb
    mark: out there in the world,
or within, before, very long ago,
or again, after and projected forward,
        like the swallow's incision,
twist: and a hole in time
            from which all comes to birth:

gate / gate / paragate / parasamgate
        matter, all hail
    wisdom, all hail—

Eyes of diamond. The look. The ashes. And: the cut.

NARRATIVE OF THE SPIDERS

For Asa Benveniste

I

The spider, as I dial a number,
hanging in the air beside me, moving with slow
exploring at the air her long forelegs, climbing the air,
the invisible hair she has spun out
of her own body, swimming an invisible sea,
where is she going, seemingly *up* to me,
and yet perhaps for her some other travel—
the spider sailing her own world,
along her own tracks
in latitudes she alone understands.

The irony—that I should have become
father to a house of spiders
as if I'd had innumerable daughters
spun from my mind alone.
No cranny in the house but has
its spider: they even nest behind the pictures
and inside books. In my own paths
I come upon them suddenly: not all the education
I've tried to give myself in their regard
prevents that shudder at their sight, and yet,
how calm they are at their navigation
and sleeping in their havens!

And it is not as if they were the large
tropical horrors I've known elsewhere, squatting like
disembodied hands on beds, or curling legs around
a windowsill: the stage-shy ballerinas. They are small
for the most part, and probably do little harm
to others of their kind within the house. Though
I have caught, in a glass, one black, to put it out,
and then a white, and suddenly, there was, there were not two,

but one black spider crouching in the glass. We must know
our thoughts, which goes with which,
and which will eat the other like a witch.

Fall. Great lines in the sky, thick and black,
as if drawn with the brush of a Japanese master,
constantly rearranging themselves over the fields,
making for South, yet with many a curve,
as if in sleep, or in desire for sleep, to wheel and land,
the whole long V of them, on some round pond,
or down the length of the sea-longing river.
Their ways are also set apart. Their noise is the most
mysterious the night knows, they conjure travel,
essence of movement. Above the house, out in the fields,
and further out into the hungry world,
some part of mind will always go with them, will be forever
traveled in their flight. As if a web of flyways in the night
covered the earth with programs. Process of their flight,
and process of the poem now made one, an ancient ritual
haunting like movement to me, come to rest.

Now the geese gone. Whereas, within the house,
within the mind, as I would criticize
the notebooks I've not written, and the poems
time has not had me for — these galley slaves, the spiders,
weaving who knows what silks and what brocades
I might in other voices weave, if I could find
the whole plan of their movement, in and out of season,
and when they will appear on a calm night, and not appear
on nights of rain when most to be expected. Syntax of fright,
clearing the way for knowledge. Which can't be fear,
is that not so, and which can only be the beauty of my daughters
as they are born, mine as they trick to dress,
mine as they die, their frail legs closed at last
around the bitter heart that could but father them,
and then leave them to fate, the cold night, or the broom.

II

The sunglasses I had lost all weekend
found at last at the bottom of my satchel
on which everything I had in the world was piled,
broken at the bridge. Glasses cannot break worse.
The voice of Alegría saying
"you no longer need dark to look at light."

And there is too much in the world
that cannot be married, or conjunct, or cemented in union
of any kind. How shall I then take the pure light
from my faithful, lifelong friend beside the bed
telling me to recognize myself in it and not fear,
and how not fall headlong, past all the brides,
lovers, fellows, acquaintances, down to the last
slip of the lizard's feet on the greasy tree,
over the skull and through the eyes
into the world of spiders?

Expecting the great spider at the mind's edge
to come like a telephone-call in the silent house,
suddenly, among the empty walls, along the bare rafters
and be so large she will engulf the house
like a call engulfs silence, changing biography,
bringing the future into life. Alegría said
"Mother." I said: "No, daughters." The Spider
which will be death—and will be also love.

My body cannot digest my soul tonight and I am left
a house of winds. "It is not necessary" Alegría said
"to cut the string of the kite when it explores the sky,
but merely to get used to the lengthening of the string
and all the places it goes." And the string
trembles to a thousand voices like a harp
with but one string. The harp with a thousand strings
is of no use to me; it is broken at the bridge like
my glasses. The kite has gone to meet its fellows in the sky.
Winds sing in the wires of the old plane,
two officers in formal dress are not height-sick, one

bellows into the other's ear through a megaphone,
the pilot calmly taking his suggestions. "Cut off the engines"
Alegría said "and took me through my fears one by one,
closed throttle, dived perpendicularly, surfed on clouds,
made me feel my body weightless, brought in the radio
to elucidate the voices of the clouds."

"And below the sea, there was a blue crab,
weaving a blue, plastic-like substance out of its tail
which then became a shell or imperial palace
the mad blue weaver lived in. Took my camera out
to find the crab I'd seen, but could not do so
and the old fisherman I'd left behind, who'd lived
many a higher life in vain and now had chosen this
to watch for men, he laughed: the grin took out his face
he laughed so much when I returned to port."

III

Uneasy, in the slip of making, yet thought for once
moving to its appointed end like a hunter.
The voices outside have sounded for three days
and have been woven into one skein. The skein is inward
now, sinking into the sea like a crab, and the sound
falls into deeper and deeper blues under the waves.
Blue line on a deep blue bed. The line follows,
among the ten thousand things of the sea, picking out
unerringly and, though I do not know it with the reel,
those things which match the discourse. Alegría sings
with bright eyes in the mind, it is the eyes that sing.

I have feared movement all my life, feared walking, feared
dancing also, feared height and depth, the air, the sea
and the path before me. Did I fall once, this fall, or in
some other fall? As I saw my daughter once,
sprawled on the floor when she was very little
— and the sudden howl as she dropped from the bed unseen
to be found on the floor? I fear the spiders
because they are there without having appeared to come

where they now are, which is: not up in the sky, but here,
in the house with us. They are my movements, those
I've not moved, but moved nevertheless, through passage
of this time I am allotted. I fear my daughters,
my actions, the blind women moving through the poem
that cannot come to birth until their mother is exhausted.
They are spiders, in delicate blue dresses, they are crabs,
they are not yet birds of air in the indigo night.

Do the birds achieve? Watch the birds move, on the wing,
perching, or feeding now among the molluscs of the pond.
Can you imagine a bird, relaxing in the grass, one knee
over the other, smoking a cigarette, let's say inactive?
The passion for achievement, to tear it from a life, impossible.
Though nausea attend it—impossible still.
Once, I found a web at the door, moving slightly in the morning
wind and destroyed it. By evening, the web had been
woven again exactly as before. I was so moved, I left it.
Destroyed. Nature is careless. Build now. It is but life.

NARRATIVE OF THIS FALL

For Robert Duncan

I do not ask for the rain to come down.
Silence. We begin with the silence and then, softly,
the rain comes down, not to argue, not to educate,
but to fall.

The light has been left on upstairs.
Downstairs. This is where
the writing materials are, where I write,
and the light upstairs is as much there
for returning unto
as it is there to enable it to fall, downstairs.

The light is below us, underfoot. It has come down
in the shape of leaves from the Norway Maple,
to argue the price of gold. Gold has not any price
when set beside these leaves. This gold will be
a short time, before it turns to dust,
first solid dust, then less and less solid,
though sand lasts a long time. That lasting is not
what we are asking here, but the price of a moment,
the price of pure yellow, unalloyed. The leaves
are not lying flat — taken leaf by leaf —
and there are several thousand leaves,
but together, they are lying flat as a carpet.
One could think of hands, cupped over each other,
or extended, with fingertips touching. They are a bother
only to birds, who wear hats of leaves
as they scrabble for seed. The light
is below us underfoot as we dance.
Looking up at the trees, I can see their fingers
whose hands I could not see
among the leaves when they were on high.
I am a king of ignorance
trying to look down from the stairs of light
at the floor below. If there is a center

to that floor, none of the dancers upon it
know where the center is.

Some men spend their lives speaking
as if they knew the center of the floor
and the exact location in the ceilings
whence that light floods down
upon each particular inch of floorboard.
I can get no information from the walls,
indeed I wonder whether there is a room around this floor
which might have walls. Nor are the dancers
in the open air as they are when among leaves.
Dancing. That was the name they had for it
in the old days, though now it would be called
circumambulation. Which supposes a center.
Which cannot be found.

I am asking certain voices
which seem to fall from on high
and which are not mine that I can recognize,
lodged into my ears from the side as it were,
although there are no walls—asking the voices whether
they know of any center to this floor.
And they answer me in certain tongues,
which although I know a good many tongues,
and those among the most ancient of tongues,
I know not the provenience of these.
Dictation. Even the machine I type on
is singing tonight, with a siren hum
trying to drown out the voices. It is clear
that I will have to inhabit this might-be room
a long time
before the center, if there is one, is revealed.

We have a compost of exasperated dissent
in the place where the fresh leaves should be
and which will see no leaves
until next Spring. Break the rhythm
is the next instruction. Manipulate
the underhand or, more correctly, the underfoot.

I stretch up to no purpose. They shall say to me,
I know, that my voice is a singing one
and that I run the cicada's blood.
If this were the place for sources,
I would argue that no specific blood runs in these veins.
I will have no Chinas here, nor Tibets,
nor Guatemalas, nor Egypts. And I give up
the beautiful scarves falling into the sea
as slowly as the years of my life falling down
this trench of what I am to be.
Even in speaking of them,
singing of them as I do here, I give them up.
They have not, before this, provided the clue
to the presence of the center, thus I deem them
useless. The only odyssey I know
is the rain from the high sky to the low,
via a multitude of intermediate skies,
losing color as it comes down, turning
transparent, losing its voices even,
becoming very silent as it touches earth,
briefly as in an acquaintance's kiss.
On the leaves it makes a little more noise,
but only a little. I know of men
who are in love with machines:
talking machines and singing machines and even
silent machines. They are the kings
of the moment, and beside my ignorance,
their ignorance is like a golden knowledge.

Others erect a Babylon of rain, driving it
up into the skies again through all the layers,
and the rain takes on their color and their voices,
until we have a Babel out of the Babylon,
beside which no harps can be hung
since there are no willows. But I will have
no Judea here either. I will silence the sources.
Sources. Silence. The light still on upstairs.
I could go back upstairs, the night is still young,
listen to the voices I know, some new ones,
and seek comfort from that. I could go

to California, or Alaska, I could travel. I could try
telling you of glaciers and mountains,
lake-formation, the marching to and fro of ice-sheets.
Or of whales at sea, humps rising
like islands each time they breathe,
sharks waiting for their blood to fall
when they are wounded. Or of populations
starving the length of the Sahel
which is the length of the arms of the world's body.
We have not enough tears to shed for the Sahel,
we have not even one tear to shed for the Sahel.
I doubt we have a tear for ourselves. The syntactic Sahel.
They ask me often why I love the desert
and I say that the sand is under the sea I love
and I must love the sand.

If this could be . . . an inhabitation. If this could be
like the dead coming to life again and having
affairs with me between the sheets, I would say yes.
If my friends could come down from their portraits
arranged against this wall, and inform me of their actions,
of the joy in their writing, the midnight hours
burning in splendor round their heads, and they were saying
things that would lead me toward the center of this fall,
I would say yes. If their souls
could come out of their bodies, out of their mouths
and ears let us suppose, or out of their navels,
or even out of their cocks and cunts, and say
what makes their pupils round, their irises
color of gold a certain moment in the dusk, then yes.
It is not as if we had no time
for miracles. This boat I lie in
like the sun on the sea going down into death,
this boat floating on the floor of the ocean
a thousand fathoms below this floor, and the whole world
away from my two ears, the whole extent of it
still declares little.

There is a hole in my tongue. In its center.
There are many holes in my mind, my mind is like a sieve.
The soup which is to keep me alive today
falls through my tongue: I have no nourishment.
I bring my right hand up to my mouth
and speak as if in asides to the other side.
The side from which the voices come, but it can be
the two sides. Confusion. We shall have confusion here
whether we wish it or not. The smoke
rises into my eyes, it is the only thing to rise
in the whole poem. I shall go to my dear one upstairs
and tell her I carry her happiness in my voice
as I would carry corn to broadcast. To scatter seed
in this fall of the year is foolish. Yet we scatter.

I have borrowed this lover from my friends
and will return her when they require it.
One of my friends, no matter which one,
has driven a stone into my central eye. I am lord
of the empire of downstairs unquestionably. With the pain
I see the magnificent crotch of my lover rise
into the light, fire burning there among my fountains.
With the odor of pine and scorched manure she burns,
with alcohol, with opium and broiled meat,
queen of the perfumes of the mountain peoples.
She falls to shoals of fish below the hills at sea,
alive among the fossils in old sands. She is clothed
in leaves. She never frets. She dances.

The snow will come soon. Winter. Or perhaps
there will be a carpet of sunlight on the naked ground.
There may be a mist over the river where I live,
a fishing boat in which I lie and dream.
Sufficient be it to take the gold into the house now,
to express it in the form of a green plant.
The green plant on my desk before me is a Swedish ivy:
it grows like riot.

I will give you tea
at this table, or coffee, or wine. I will cook for you
at this table and entertain you with mirth
or conversation. You will tell me of times
gone and to come. You will have no voice
but it be peripheral, certainly you will not bring me news
of the hidden kingdom in the center of the floor.
There's a great deal of love in our relationship.
I will weigh your scholars in the palm of my hand,
saying they correspond to this or that knowledge
I have accumulated over the years, and I will tell you
whether their books are true or false. But of the floor,
I will not say a word and you will be unable to likewise.

the microcosm

IN THE SCRIBNER ROOM, PRINCETON LIBRARY

You opened your arms wide
bared your teeth in one smile
opened your arms wide
and your beautiful frontage
under cereal shirt
opened wide also
your breasts Apollo's apples
Hesperides your waist
with its sweating fountains
penumbra of Nile
out of dark Egypt
into American sun
with golden grasses
honey and pepper perfumes
apricot juices

And all day you smiled like that
your eyes chasing your lips
your lips chasing your eyes
neither quite catching up
I wanted you a lot
on chairs   tables   or floors
or up against the stacks
our scholarship melting
gods coming in now and then

Evening we were tired of sex
though we hadn't had any all day
I still wanted you inked
into the groundwork of American Lit
you chased last weekend's breakthrough
saying fuck me to that place again

Our house is built on solid theses now

SVAIRYE

All day   you on my fingers
       and in memory
you finding cancer
       in the bed's battlefield
eyes unbuttoned to the heart
       your voice saying svairye svairye
the great god of giving and being given
   your forgiveness for all my nameless sins
you are not violent

     in the home of your mouth

ON THE WAY TO GREEN MOUNTAIN

For me, she is the cornerstone of the first heaven
and I miss her to the roots of my life

Where we lay down in rich loam
richer than any found by men

grew stalks of sons, flowers of daughters
the place of being born and coming back to die
the seat of our thrones abandoned on the waves

where we loved like children
like the first twins
& knew each other completely before beginning

And I had to go out one day
into the wild imperfect trees beyond the garden
the angel slapping my back as I passed

so that a metal hand to this very day
pushes me out of every new-found refuge
excluding me from every forest

The compass has long since ceased to swivel
as I travel in all directions together
searching for the first shore for lack of which

no other shore has any edge or meaning

KADMON'S SISTER

Where the fire played
blonde over water
a flame deep red
burns on the surface now

she stands in mind
her head turned to the right
sharp in the ocean breeze
        her curls playing about her
her head on fire

her hands
        one imagines her hands
parting her thighs before her
low in the photograph
enters with gratitude
the haven there

she gives such welcome
as one imagines from angels
but with a lust so friendly
a child could benefit
breaking into his manhood
and her soft speech
        raises the mind toward
her greeting mouth

sweet ruddy girl of earth
Kadmon's bright sister
stand like a bow in mind
slender and throbbing
I give you gratitude
and brotherly affection
you fuck like incest
and come like fall

light everywhere the red around you

THE MICROCOSM

For P.R.T.

The land is larger than itself
breathing beyond its normal girth
in the light-hearted air

it takes a bird even of prey
many wingbeats
seemingly still to cover it

fields heave as if with voices
throats distending to throw words
ejaculate from all the furrows

the mole has fallen like a star
into the peopled world
pushing the lawn up into rills

the everresting rose
puts down her roots to boil
swells to a cloud of flowers

between tree fingers
a telescope achieves the sky
quietly like a confident husband

and at the climax of the firmament
ringed with a crown from another sphere
Saturn alone is spinning on itself

in the wavering summer light

birdscapes with seaside

In memory of Ivan Morris

*"... & the philosophical light around my window is
now my joy; may I be able to keep on as I have thus
far!..."* —HÖLDERLIN 12.2.1802

It must be to tears
  to the world, dissolving,
it must be to terror,
  inhibitions of thought,
it must be to paralysis
      to the blood quenched
  hands fallen asleep
         that it's due—
I had forgotten them:
  and here like clocks come home
       the amenable birds

::

as long as heart beats
blood diffuses through life
       pacing cold village—
    there by the creek
       half ice, half water
    brushy stands of seeds
and an attack
    of cardinals, six or as many,
(in the seeming flock):
    rush up the ventricles,
      seizure of sun
        smiling invisibly

::

seed
   in itself
      though one year old
still not dead
   breeding very small worms
for the crested tits:
   cat-cradle in air
as they criss cross above
      the seed dispenser
& I wd. have sworn the seed was dead
if there hadn't been, in my mouth,
   a smile sick of repression
yessing the birds today
     back to this hope, this charity

::

at the very stale
term of all mind,
   old cat dragging its tail along
      like I drag my feet
against the work:
         the craft of thought
   over the abyss
        below this work—
all my years surfacing, all these
          existences
over-familiar with me,
people I've known
never go back to
food like the memory these birds
have no idea they issued from—
   angels / at x per feeder

::

all back
despite late start so
     bad for business:
the tit forementioned,

purple finch,
gold, chickadee,
        at ground the
whitethroat, junco,
cardinal & jay, and,
        at his drilling,
the woodpecker.
                Nuthatch . . .
            Where is nuthatch?
            Hatching thought.
    Missing.
Nuthatch nuthatch yourself.
    Forward from origin boy!
Nuthatch. Nuthatch damn it!
        ah, leave be

::

bird in air
        (the artist arted)
passage to the food
            under the bird,
the air opens
cupped hands hold grace
                unconcealing:
we shld. have been philosophers
I sd. the work begged doing long
ago — the work is light again —
                    flight
    to the seed taken back
hammered on branch
                    sweet core
            hungered for so,
long his & ours
            smells in the eaves

::

sublime pointlessness
of being peep
in flock of peeps
spending a year or two as bird
running to and from tidal waves
picking for cockles
spending the energy as fast as gained
all this under the immense—
so that we name it on our rest
from feeders—cloud of sea, beach, sky,
          sublimest metaphor unless
(my day in the office & yours)
really in the clearing
all is open on all else

::

blessed power
that has handed down
or caused to happen
     on this dark lake
held in winter's paws
          the class mallard,
the class baldpate,
          or the ruddy duck,
the class black duck
          und so weiter
(all of which duly recorded)
as well as the classes
          never binoculared:
     hooded merganser
comma of water speech,
     canvasback
russet exclamation,
     whistling swan
white question mark
     eyes have not opened on before
anywhere on the stage—
& that thou hast confirmed what is
congruent with its expectations

even if that be science only
                & not yet wisdom

::

the great birds of the sea
do not to the great ocean down
        & dive he would say
mostly for food
        but for eye's joy
hermit's happiness
                on this lone shore
saint to himself alone—
                but, inasmuch as
they fly in company of kin
    & never solitary
so that their time is a history
            (as we understand it)
thus, it is for the hungry in ourselves,
the humanity which is our nature,
        that, like us, toiling,
they down to smelt & worm,
their lovely passage a banality
            to fill the belly
they and we must march on
                if we are to grow
legs, wings of willing

::

the birds
    home from the sea as we are
each in their turn
        draw every branch
in its turn
        to the feeder—
            garden is
drawn
    together, gathered in: *un-*
                less

the whole garden
　　　　has been gathered first
　　back from the ocean
　　　　　(be it known to you)
& no bird flies from branch,
　　no branch springs bird
　　　　　　　to center:
　　no rain is water
　　　　that is not wine,
　　no seed flour
　　　　that is not bread,
nectar's no drift

::

the philosopher's
　　　　surface is kind
& easy & it goes
　　　　through all the birds
like a flu—
　　　　how come each bird sounds
unlike itself this morning,
　　　　pecks at the feeders
in unaccustomed ways?
　　perhaps they sing
or chirrup in the memory
of the birds of the great sea
　　　　so far behind us now
at anchorage,
　　　　glimpsed for a moment only,
their noise
mere dream as that sea's self
speaks & outreaches
　　　　　　sail setting sail

::

at the twelfth hour
　　wind round the house
a mindless ocean,

156

police cars
    radios blaring
(jays & crows)

    jumpy for action but
busting what? preventing what
robbery of imbecile robberibles?

in the huge dark
    we lie, wet worms of light,
for spirit birds to feed on

meantime the smallfry:
    what do they say to all this dying
waiting for breakfast

    as the moon turns and sparks
unforgettable stars
            in the frostrimmed bushes

In the spring rain death's dust rubs off
the bird who has been hidden all winter
like a fire which conspires under embers
needing only a master's touch to flare:
so the gold, understood there all along,
invests the bird at present hardly conscious
of this encroaching beauty. He fans air
under his weight and, more like a sorcerer's
apprentice now, pleasures himself, a boy,
eating the last of winter's grain.
Then notes one morning in his new discretion
he is of the same substance as the sun.

alashka

(a joint work with janet rodney)

FROM: THE GROUND OF OUR GREAT
ADMIRATION OF NATURE

I

The poet as the sole
                remaining speaker
          can now,
the whole, grown beyond reason,
     still speak of whole, but, now
as certain is to probable
                     in other languages,
          the wonder—
mind shock: incompatibility,
                     admiration,
wonder ever recurring despite
                the loss of doubt
     in that respect (considered as "beauty"):
her arms swimming, as if through water,
the frontal surge of breasts, like frozen
     breathing
          at the apex—
          but / in fact / in air—
"too much language, too much language,
     too many games, now, with the language":
our positions almost lost
          unless it is not water
     she comes through, at the apex
                but air
                residence of the purpose, the
     seeing,
          need for us still in the blood of the air
                so thin now, leukemic ...)
the mermaid song
     her tail, our desire, such a comet
                among air's trees:
     as if lungs were still
as if causally / pretending only
                     but *required?*

IV

Close to
            suspecting in some part
that wide and utter freedom, stroke of wing
                across the emptiness,
feather against the cloud
                tip of the void
forcing the lock
   like a key
      to fly beyond, into
the world we have before us now
                our eyes opened
on our hands before us,
                body below us
feet touching ground
   and it is:
         what this earth? what, this
loam so fertile, it has a name, it is
         recorded in the early books
                / is it not?
   books which still speak
         union of dead and live
      where they have not let us go quite yet
            into the wings,
      the screens, and hidden corridors
of the clouds—
   suspecting in some part
            that wide and utter freedom
We hear of somewhere, and are   /   so close to   /   sometimes
                it is almost as if
   (the great bones hug our souls)
somewhere at last we could
                sweet virgin land
   so nearly
         touch it . . .

VII

Archaeology of Nature:
            memorials
of ancient mighty desolations
            man had no part in:
    mammoth-rut below starlight,
whale among icebergs,
                    the purpose of our genitals,
    organization of love,
whereby all created things come to birth
            (and shall we say
            petrification being of
the order of A. of N., not
            history natural,
            stone has no say in purpose?)
But the very organ
set those same whale leaping through Tongass
            we saw in admiration
as the sweet product of our ancient patience,
            has been, time past among,
            (among the icebergs)
a stone as well,
    so wood among the trees
with which the soul-cage used to breathe
a stone as well:
            if there be any trees
                    in these cold regions.
The mind
    says it will do this:
        evolve from stone
                with all its gorgeous colors
setting the tundra quietly on fire
        beyond the night,
(little sparks of fire, like
    love in flame when life
        most hopelessly devours us).
We have come a long way
from the familiar eastern shores
                    to the ground

of our great admiration of nature
and we watch the grays
weave with the silvers and the golds
and the sands, and the grays again, out to sea
beyond the polar ice
which is the blue of angels' faces,
    when they are cold—as we say:
    COME INTO THE HOUSE OF OUR LIFE
    ye that have hugged the bones
    whose rib-cage is the whale
    that swallowed the prophet
    of the mighty sea. Crosses, crosses
now, above Point Hope, the shamans dead,
imagination buried
under the oval freezure,
                the petrified milk-drop
the bones, jutting into the sky like the teeth
of an animal more immense than the whale . . .

    Hold, hold to your patience
beyond the immemorial angers
        and she will fly into your poem,
            who are there
wearing her mask today, & breasts, beating her drum.

NARRATIVE OF THE GREAT ANIMAL

Denali was our greatest animal.
We might   never have seen it, doubted
all reports, never realized
                    why it was unmistakably
lord of America.
                        It rose, when it rose,
two whole days
            out of surrounding mountains
                    like the sun's ghost
after a burial at sea,
                    like the white whale
out of the sea
            defining all else immediately.

Almost a painting.
    That unreal: as when they say: "postcards,"
                                    etc.
                (or "travel poster.")
Archetype of all mountains,
                behind the mind, lurking,
no: they say of a *beast* "lurking"
            and we talk of gods.
Always there, against: the epiphany.
                White ship of space, rootless,
suspended from the clouds.
                Sometimes, the whole sky gray,
the crown, floating by itself in the heights / or /
                clouds on its face: recessing it
into immeasurable farness,
                or lifting it (the mountain) / depressing it,
according to the play of cloud.
                A RESURRECTION.
                            From the dead,
from the death of our senses, in its shroud,
which is also a wedding gown:
                bride/bridegroom

in one plenitude.
Knowing, or not, the plenitude: there is
                    no other question.
(That we could have been, again, encamped,
with most of humanity at the foot, and spent
days,   days, weeks even,   and not seen it/
as so many, coming all this way,
on little money, their poor lives spent,
at the gates now, and, *still*, not seen it:
this   beats   all   matters   of   election,
and Mallarmé's absence, or Kafka's gatekeepers.)

                When, thus, it rose,
and we, disbelieving, who had said
    all along the way
                "Is *this* Denali,
and then this, and this, and this—
                    since there is no end to
    the mountains
                    but, patient, there being always a step below
    suspect perfection,
                    until, at road-curve,
"Oh My God," hushed, and you not seeing yet, and then
                you also
"oh my god," in a still greater hush,
                        because, now, there was
    no possible mistaking.

                GREAT STAR OF SPACE
from the dead
    complete,
                in its motionless travels,
even then: at its destination, never yet gone
                        from earth, its
                parent. We might not

have seen it, never
                have looked on god's face
and lived (so far) to tell tales.

                        Had we not
        seen it,
        the world
        would have always
        forever thereafter,
        and its word, *logos,*
seemed smaller   because,
                after the moon, after all,
        it is never the same again:
an earthly thing has to be great indeed, perfect indeed,
                        to give that plenitude / that lack
        of argument, tells us we have
                        looked on god's face
and lived (so far) to tell tales.

And, had we not seen this,
would not have seen, either,
in any sense of the word "seen,"
since only this mountain gave the world eyes
                        and senses
to apprehend it with
        (catalogue / world model):
        the cinnamon mountains,
        all the other mountains
        in their variety,
        the heaving bears, with earth
        like Atlas on their shoulders,
        wolves, running fast as cars,
        our idiot ptarmigan, posing at roadside,
        the payroll animals, bowing as each bus passes,
        the tourists shouting . . .
                (continue at own leisure)

our—minute—preoccupations
under Denali:
   horned lark (American first)
   eagle (repeat); eagle (but immature)
   wheatear (American first)
   phalarope (American first)
   (continue as per notebook,
   list climbing, x% of total record).

        But the invisibles:
           harlequin duck (later: St. Paul)
           arctic warbler (later: Point Hope)
           golden plover (later: Shishmaref)
           ivory gull (later: Gambell)
           gyrfalcon (later: Nome) —
        all these,
        waiting for the next time,
        the world being in place now,
           no problem.
        And seen, then, again and again,
           the lord Denali,
        from Turnagain Arm, Cook Inlet,
        from the roadside, on the Fairbanks Highway,
        from the plane, out of the Pribilofs,
        as if it were a friend now,
        and reluctant to leave ...

and the great animal,
even greater than *this* animal,
(Denali god-beast,
with hips of stone,
rock haunches),
      waiting for the next occasion also
to get us before another sighting,
      another chance at this vicinity
      among the thorns and dangers of this world—
      BUT WE HAVE SEEN IT

and thus, by implication, also the other
as dark as this is bright . . .

Cloud of mosquitos,
Splat: blood on hands, face, clothes
wolf / moose / bear / bird blood perhaps,
John Doe from Texas, or Oklahoma blood,
                                    ("the animals")
What a merger in the sight of the whole!

                    Outside the Park, every signpost in Alashka is
                            riddled with bullet holes,
                    the land should have never seen people
                                        this blight on it

                    back into "civilization" . . .

II

We could not remember its form
                        (the mountain, woman now)
dropped from high cloud
                    on memory,
mind's waters/
                    ripples growing dark
        covering the imprint
lying dormant,
                    imagination failing
        this whole year.

                    Year of miracles:
to have carried the mold all these months
                    in the magnitude of space.
Now we had traveled to the edge
of the procession of peaks and valleys
would lead us to her flanks,

trip to the rim of vision,
pointing always through the overcast,
        remembrance of . . . a possibility
as a heliotrope fathoms the hidden sun.

Deep in waters, the mountain lay
wrapped in her veils and promises
ready to give herself from the feet up.

Foothills, an artist's workshop,
ochres, siennas, ambers,
draw the eye up to lose itself in blue heights,
dream of her radiance above our heads
weaving imperfect shades,
happy as children allowed to play
until light fades on hills around,
dwarf world of plants clinging to the tundra,
spreading outward like mats, sad as love-pangs,
wildflowers, short of summer warmth,
flickering energies on the bank,
        mosquito-murder in the greens . . .
        "Lady, breathe your wind,
        move the dwarf-plants
        upon their fragile stems
        above our heads."

From the movement of
        a number of nearby stars
                        we imagine that
a mountain becomes ours   from the depths
        conceived as a bride
                        from among the dead:
how stone mixes,
    slime firing in the kilns,
peaks claw skyward in some paroxysm,
folds settle in silence as for years
snow falls, cools into ice, flakes shrink,

lace tips melt
                    and

eyes move
with a rush of birdwing
to see it—equanimity
                    wings go, eyes stay
fuse with the contours of her limbs
                    as the hills shake,
knees flex, elbows angle
                    under the lapping tide and,
        suddenly
the great herds
emerge from the valley's end
hoofmarks on snow, churned up silks,
animals pouring like cataracts through passes,
columns of swaying antlers
                    cresting on skylines,
tatters of velvet like an army's banners
flying from pikes and lances,
the water mixed with snow and mud, waves
tan and grey as far as eye can see,
no start, no end—earth moves,
migrating North, driven by the shuffle of season,
nothing is steady underfoot, eyes quake
as the whole landscape floods.

        In the wind
                    a fawn is dropped
        arrests the tide
    but momentarily,
                    stopping the robe an instant
from sliding altogether
                    to leave the mountain bare.

        Will the sun
through interplay of cloud and weather

touch the mountain with a bridal flush
      or will she tonight
           recline in quiet grays,
               a fading diva,
         whole camp as one
      facing in her direction
as she silently reads
        without stage effect
            the poem of her life?

We   both   here
in this process
        neither the outer
nor the inner suffer,
    the mountain
shaping our minds,
         and later, as the mind
gathers and shapes the mountain,
            never loss.
In the dark,
        animal tides ripple still,
the night will not quench that flow but take it
         like a sea
from one end of the earth to the other.
           And not a moan,
not a wind whisper, but silence
           itself made motion
     on memory.
Gives the mountain back itself
     in marble tones
refraining from destruction
        of lesser things.

Until at last
light on flank and crown,
        and death all lowered,
she stands revealed
wherever we would find ourselves within her country.

Time speeds us to encounter,
(human voices fading into the background)
             the whole range
                          burns with white fire.
         Star among stars
whose radiance in the end
             comes to rest among men,
the taiga carpet receiving her,
             ponds and lakes catching her flare
                          on this last day,
voices of birds and grasses
             crisscrossing in the night,
low hum of insects in the hells,
                          memory stirring from its den,
         to try once more her storage.

III

God   /   Goddess

    Bride   /   Bridegroom

entailing,
         in each our attitudes,
the best in me, which might be woman,
in you, which might be man.
         How will they tell,
who hear the poem of its life (the mountain's)
         which verse of it wrote which
and, following, who ended the stanza
                          when eyes fell closed
in the dazzled tent
   whose blues and greens
                          we baptized at its knees?

As the light recedes
and takes from this frail universe
                        all terms of life,
        (leaves us in darkness
        most any planet could rush and occupy,
        ourselves, waking to morning in another world
                    with no familiar maps) —
what a disconsolate place we inhabit
which could change out of recognition,
taking the seals of bride and bridegroom both
out of creation overnight, and leave us prey.

                        The stars
move like a tide over sleep,
        the cosmos,
                its peaks and seas
        in a procession:
                    suddenly   (as one might put it)
                    the great herd of stars
                    moving across the night   in silence
        without a moan, without apparent wind to move them
                losing themselves completely
                                over the rim . . .

In the afterdark
        memory beginning to slip,
                            female thoughts,
        male thoughts,
                the small child thoughts,
                                like bannerets,
all going out at once, with starlight
                and the mountain also,
        reluctantly,
                (its rock
                        hardly awake to move, but
going over the edge also
                        and our storage
                                without retrieval.

Knowing, or not, the plenitude: there is
                              no other question.
And, without forcing it,
                    the profundity.
            I collect stones, you
make your list of birds—we dredge
                              the well of records.
When the page is full for the day,
                  we can make love: this turn
will take us into manhood, us to womanhood,
                                        earth

shifting again underfoot
as if the hooves migrated through our knees.
                  This foursome
        of the implicit in each,
                  bridal to the other,
and then the total other,
                  strange at trail's end,
        of whatever sex,
                or of no sex whatever
(if the stars indeed have gone over and the world
                seethes with a new idea or two)
                        placing us both in question
                        and all identity.

This has to be a move,
retrieving the mountain,
in all its aspects,
translating   /   an exhibition:
                  the massive power now
against
    the pity of it.
                The smallness, meanness,
        insignificance
                  of all of it.
                  Like destroying this land.
                  This culture, however meagre.
                  Making a laughing stock
        of this humanity.

Ending Alashka
before it has begun.
              Deep in the well of darkness,
small flowers stir.
              They look at us, as a flower in Blake might do,
for a moment,
              the whole fate of our universe hangs on them:
                        whether tomorrow,
they are picked or not,
                    trodden under foot or not,
                                browsed or not,
by the tide of cattle.

                "How far we are from each other
                how close we are

                like a flower
                which cannot see itself
                and finds no mirror it can use
                in the clouded sky"

IV

At the moment of strain,
                    resolution
pushing up clouds off the valley floors
                        makes
out of cloud a mountain—
                    (in our dreams
had we seen whale
                above the waves
or waves themselves
                their blades of darkness?)

                At the moment of strain,
        the killing time—

as if a sudden intruder,
in the middle of the poem
                    were to walk in oblivious,
or if even you
                    were to touch me now
when the whole weight of it hangs in the balance,
or if this machine,
                    unable to bear the speed
of our attack on the mountain,
                    were to stumble, break down,
and lose the guiding thought—
                    so that the peak
could not loom above the cloud
                    as if it really were
in place, and not some play:
imagination under cloud /

                    play   /   gamble

                    and one were sick
with a lurch of breath
                    into throat,
bile over tongue, nerves
                    shredded for the rest of the year:
        for memory
        would have blown connections
        and would not know
                    what lay behind the cloud.
(Facing north,
or what we thought was north, waiting,
                    for the mountain to come out
thinking there was something petty about the foothills,
but making nothing of it,
                    (experts now),
                    the mountain, hours later,
        like a trickster yet again,
                    suddenly coming out of the northwest,
taking our breath away:
                    immensity—
                but with a partial tallness,

the summit in cloud now,
the waistline open, but higher than
all height our memory had cradled.

IS IT THE MOUNTAIN LIES BEHIND THE CLOUDS, OR IS THE SUN . . . . ?
OR LOVE, THAT MOVES THE SUN AND OTHER STARS . . . . ?
SOMETHING UNSAID AS YET . . . . ?

At the moment of strain,
                    sleep meets waking
under the eyelids;
                    the animals
flow in their tides over the hills,
the reins held firmly by the stars,
                            washing themselves
on a dark tide
                    over night-rocks:
                            thought itself
a swell within the skull,
                    linked to that movement
(backs of dolphin and whale)
            as if some stillness
                        were the enemy.

        We have put up today
our defenses
            against oblivion.
                        The mountain has put up
its longer argument.
        All definitions
hang in the balance.
                    We are content
        to rest in every case.

the desert mothers

FLIGHT FROM THE MOUNTAINTOP

For Isac Chiva

"Aber Freund! wir kommen zu spät. Zwar leben die Götter,
Aber über dem Haupt droben in anderer Welt."

—HÖLDERLIN

1

Running off the mountain:
        billow of air,
ground drops below peak,
multicolored sails swerving
        above the valley:
not us flying those wings
    but flown by them.
    Tangle unraveled—
    the compelling
    drag on the bird . . . feet and legs in lime,
    beak in his own thick blood,
        needles sticking through feathers,
        all that behind us.)
Now: arrows, spears, lances,
        columns, towers of air:
        victory headless at the crest,
        yet throat spouting song,
        stump bare and hardly bleeding.

    In their dreams men are
    (gods)
    he had said,
        in reflection: SLAVES.
    Ground is philosophy,
            the hospital—
    but the air
        six thousand feet above the valley:
    you can't think of wreckage.
    In his flight

remembered the isle of light,
how one morning

had borrowed father's wings,
strapping them on as if for combat, and had
neighbored the sun awhile in soaring lovelike
and free with birds, angels and all manner of
musical spheres, planets and meteors . . .

In their dreams (he had sd.) men were
        alike.
Dumb bums below, his life was bound up with
        in scalding slavery,
failed to recognize
his cataract out of the morning sky,
           blood like the lightest wine
dissolved in sun and aether.
           He could not have been
salvaged out of that air in any shape
recognizable to man, beast, god,
once he had started falling and
you could not have looked into his eyes
since the sun had taken them quite out.
           But his mind from then on—we are told
in his final speech—what a hoard that was
of incisive tools, and how well he knew
what he wanted around him and what
had to be trashed, like old shoes,
           outside his door.

2

"in the dream,
the glide descends in spirals
down to the extremity of my country
from which a ship will take you
        to the farthest peninsulae
of all other imagineable countries.

It is a winter there
                I had previously thought
                                unfathomable."

"In deepest winter
            coldest things calm most.
Causing the mind to desist from raving and to still
inexhaustible choice that is making us all mad.
My gods, how I pity you in this iron age
and want silence now, from now on, always,
and shall not speak to you anymore, nor fly with you,
holding your hands in the sun, protecting your wings,
shielding the delicate wax on your shoulders
from his deadly bite."

"What it had occurred to me to say
concerned the birds of deepest winter in my country,
out of a north larger than memory,
perhaps full of mountains off whose peaks they flew,
which had now congregated for my eyes' pleasure
on the border black lakes of my country:
all that sludge on the lakes like sick thought
sensing its own destruction.
            The end as I had predicted
        (that silent end full of bombardments)
of intellect."

"Is not the metaphor of our indited clarity
that exquisite bird, part white, part black,
whose very head, the pattern of the head,
                is our question mark?
I forget (deliberately)
birds of one color
even the great
            ghost trampler of women,
or the black lout of the sea in all his forms,
who stands for the night of the sea in all his forms,
            and has no name, or,
if you will, a multitude, no matter."

"—Your Majesty, my pilots sick today,
unfit for battle. They will not *think*
at the controls, they are dangerous.
I remember the country of the living,
                    how they spoke in tongues,
the orders they gave, and the surrenders.
    I was granted today the order of silence
    Already I don't remember speech."

"Speech, I think, was like that very wide
                        river behind my house
very beautiful in the cold air of winter,
                    the blues especially,
carrying the perspective of all human things,
                    whether you looked
back to the source of the river, or down to the sea.
                        It is time
perhaps to move inland and look for walls.
                    A tower perhaps.
My wife, held back by her own husband always
        (an air-traffic controller)
might not get around to making it with me.
I don't know whether it will be possible to fly again:
    my flights may be long and impressive,
        but will not be visible anymore.
                Je suis hors concours.
These are the elegies, which is: a search for
the origin which does not belong to our deathless order.
And yet we are commanded to purify mankind
and the sentinel number I have posited as
characteristic of the nightly eras of the earth."

3

And let me add
that if it were not for my own extreme sympathy with him—
I mean he who has delivered the poem to you this way,
I could not have spoken like this
nor begun to tell you

that in America we now have
       a dreampath again, or spirit quest if you will,
departing every day from the mountain top—
                        billow of air underwing
      ground lost below height,
          although it is not certain that anyone will look
at the finest flyers as they perform in the blue sky,
in the thunderhead sky with tones of copper or iron
over the misted ground at zero/zero—
          whether they soar beyond the sun
      or collapse into the sea below
          or fix the shape of their outspread arms and legs
on the crumpled ground
                   (slaves to reflection),
     the middle of their bodies pulverized
        by the effort of flight
and the order of angels closed for the time of this era
              to any candidate whatsoever.

ENTERING INTO THIS

For J.R., in no way differently

Granted that
         life is
   irremediably *dukkha*:
               dis-comfort, dis-satisfaction,
Dis, in this life above ground
      which is mostly shadow, in which light
must be introduced, dab at a time:
      fingertip, brush of eyelid, chest hair,
aura round the generation machine in its upstanding
            jus/tice—and finally that light
so hard won is shaded, stroke by stroke, by the same
      pencil in its pride of darkness,
drawing you down to Dis in this life . . .
               Whoever promised
all floors were different: "in my mansion many rooms"
but did anyone say, this room, that, will be a garden?
did anyone promise? Did one say tulips? roses? maple
just before snow: the ultimate in fire? Or ever say
snow—whose white defeats those strokes for blind days?
      Then, if you, yes, I thought if you would, grant
such a premise, we could rest from hope in the definite,
      you and I—this hope knowledge would be ours
WHOLE—after the escalation. And no more climb. The
mountains are, last enough if last is any point to make,
while the world's flowers take our eyes on down
   to the canyons arush with crazy april waters—
   Where we see the great wall move at us, take us,
and we wait for it, standing stock still.

OR THAT THE PRESIDENT WOULD ABDICATE

For Shamoon Zamir

They never dreamed it.
　　　Or that the president,
discussing his wars with a general,
　　　should give one thought to a soldier,
a common man, or
　　　initiate consideration of his fate
　　　　　and, by extension,
perhaps call off the war: no,
　　　no president will talk, except of other leaders,
　　　as if to say: kings? KINGS? *what* kings?
Thrones are well-oiled, kings always protected.
　　　Now think, not even *of* the soldier,
　　　think THE soldier, the SOLDIER:
how his life beds down in the dust
　　　and he has not been asked.
That there are, oh, untold millions of soldiers,
　　　and they have not been asked.
And now, you can bring out the poems,
　　　the autumn poems especially,
color of blood—and you can swear that this time
　　　the poems will be difficult.
　　　　　　　Not to excavate,
but to bring forth:
　　　they need to be torn from their hinges.
You have been putting off this moment
　　　for most of your existence now,
　　　　　(that use of *now*) and NOW,
it is inescapable: the poem's new
　　　or else, each time, a soldier dies for it.
　　　Or that the president would die,
walk off into a grove, to be blinded there,
step up to a hill, to be hung from a cloud,
　　　slide into a gully, to be mangled by animals—
but go, GO, it would be time for him to GO.

Silence approaches,
a lonesome, ancient man.
All are gone home. You are the poet.
With silence moving toward you,
and you trying to work your throat, your voice,
the ice-blue mind.

DEATH FEAR—YET OF ANOTHER

For J.P. Auxémery

It is not a fear—
            though he is going out of his mind,
                        though his words
tumble over each other so fast,
            no idea can ever form completely,
                        and the drift, the drift is only
toward the dead and exhaustion of meaning.
It is not a fear,
            because there is no thing
                        that you can name to fear:
it is a trepidation, a war in the nerves,
            electric wires on fire in the brain,
                        reaching to the idea,
but never getting where
            you can say: ah, there it is,
                        clear, shining, the star
toward which I have always traveled,
            whose light I've seen
even though it began before my birth.
            He is MAD. It is difficult to say he is *mad*
            for to define true madness
            is no true rest.
But that
            not getting at
                        no thing that we can
name, can hold, can change
            into the star, or image of the star,
even remembrance, symbol,
            any remotest memoration of that star:
                        this is the terror, building
temples, observatories,
            as if the architecture tried to lift itself
and HE, still babbling,
            from somewhere back of where we are,
                        way back to ARCHE, of which the LOGOS, lost,

189

sustains and feeds the trepidation.
                    As if something like cancer
            were going to be announced,
and all life dissolve,
            as the crab once took my love into the sea,
                    under the deepest rock to lie,
                    as one lies on one's back
                                to be boned.
Do not worry, the friend says:
            he is not among the living,
                    this babbler.
Those people I worked with, they would sing:
            he is gone among the *Bao* (i.e. the dead)
                    Which he already speaks with,
                        is loved by, with love we cannot know.

at the western gates

FROM: JOURNAL OF THE LAGUNA DE SAN IGNACIO

Immense architecture
building in air
towers and palaces
from which their eyes look out,
star denizens
living in the heights
as they live below
and undersea
their passage through our life—
            a gentle glide
like a dream
because no thing men know
can be other than dream
      in such a world.
Whales breathing
all around us in the night
just beyond the lights,
ghost gulls
following the ship
which seems to breathe
yet never moves
against the great Pacific's
unfathomable shoulders

::

The mountains rise out of the desert
way out over Baja
the whales rise out of the sea
the mountains rise out of the sea
the whales rise out of the desert
the whales are taller than the mountains

::

There was a man one time
got buried in a whale they say,
found bed and board down there
also some breakfast,
found desk and library
and was granted extra knowledge
          (the whale a shaman they say).
          Cast from the human city,
he went down to the sea in whales
clothed with all his grave clothes
collected over the years
complete with turquoise necklace
and jadeite necklace
and one bead of jade —
his body full of sweet winds,
          he lay inside the whale
and wrote, in his death, terrible hymns
which no amount of pain
had ever torn from him,
wrenched from his mouth
          in his mind's hearing

::

Touching the skin of water
as it glides against water
slow slip of time
the black flesh gleaming like a hull
          (they call it Gray)
mottled with barnacles,
the imaginary touch
which men could have touched for centuries
          instead of the carnage)
as it took them so long
to come to the beaches
to come to the sea
to come to the mountains

::

Dazzle of light
pale mountains, pale dunes
pale clouds on pale blue skies
immense skullcap of light over the whole,
                          the sea fetching sighs
          under the skiff,
his heart
folded among the sea's pages—
                  from the depths coming up
          in musical surf
arched bow of the whale
          the vertebrae
shining through skin
circling the skiff
passing, they say,
the flukes over his head
so fast he did not see them
(though they were larger than his houseroof)
but felt the hair on his head
lie down which the wind had raised.
                  And the heart came up also
which, in its fear,
the sea had previously bound into its secrets

::

Lagoons in space
enclosed like wombs
satellites of earth,
wide mirrors receiving
the planet's music,
          star songs
in well-tuned skies.
Far out in space,
warmed by the sun,
fry, bubble, sizzle,
in silver-wrap
the celestial whales:
down drip of blubber
(deluge of calm)

turning our sphere
every sign of the zodiac
to their own favor

::

& how come no fear
in this roiling—
dragons among the waves,
behemoth   /   leviathan,
close as domestic pets?
        If they barked, I think,
as loud as their size suggested,
childhood would tower
out of all proportion,
the world's walls
would cave in,
the floor break earthquake:
I would probably not
enter this lagoon
in a battleship!

::

"Though they take me down
into the freezing wave,
though they drop me naked
to the invisible,
and I cry there
for any voice to answer—
one voice out of the void—
and no voice sounds,
while leviathan
rises from below
his mouth agape
to take me in his body,
though they kill me and cut me to pieces
to feed me to the whale:
still I sing,
still do not keep quiet,

they have a singer
on their hands
and a voice
talking, singing, praying,
they cannot quench
if only sun returns
to bless the earth like this
once in the centuries
between each of my breaths"

::

"Perhaps it is not the sea
we have witnessed
raising these whales
to the power of air
and downing them again to depths
unheard of in the history of water—
                perhaps it is the sky,
even paradise,
and these are the heavenly animals
with wings of wind and music
who have laid their image
on all earthly souls
(since nothing is forgotten)."
Father, the gate is open
        he declared on landing.
Wrote on that desk
and in that book they say
that was the oldest in the library
    within the belly of the whale:
                "these are the animals
the ancient men,
blind leading blind,
in the old days, on the old ships
with perfumed masts,
hearing the music of the sirens
                thought to be angels ..."

FROM: THE LAND SONGS

For Hans ten Berge

"Suddenly
he forgot that I was alive
& spoke of me in my presence
as if I were dead.
Reading my future
and telling me of loss.
                    Far off
a noise of breakers
through which the whale
taking apart the night with method
denied all possibility of day,
filtering star-like shrimp
through her baleen as tall as towers.
Fragments of action. Of any action"

::

"Canyons in which
I have walked on the floor of the sea
feet firm on sand,
hands
fluttering in disbelief
along rock walls,
eyes full of cholla flowers
manmillaria flowers,
the goddess-nipples
            spiky today,
nostrils cool with the odor
sunlight draws from feathery palms,
rich banks of succulents
along the interface of sand and water.
Underfoot,
stone is hard
and unforgiving as a dying prophet.
Oh, death might come now

to the ball of the eye
and take these feet
back to their golden pavements!
Out front
great walls of surf
as wide as her arms
who mothers the sea and all its creatures
among which whales play in the mind
sounding along its convolutions
and breaching into the clear air of genius:
where they cover the mother's bosom,
her naked splendor with their wings"

::

"Another sorrow.
One more defeat.
Another death.
The sea's outside,
silent waves
breathe in all other sounds.
Suddenly I meet the beauty of my poems
whom I had never seen bridal before.
I live with them as man and wife
outmarried by death only.
There is no other house"

FROM: JONAH'S SADDLE

For Michel Deguy

TWO

Whose is the divine voice,
who is mistress of whales on the other side
                    of the morning wind?
Wasting the knowledge
the rapping man might give
in order not to listen
to any other knowledge than hers.
There was clearly a marriage below that belt.
   To analyze
      what whales mean
         when he is talking merely of horses,
to translate
      horses into whales—
divine cavalcades with hoofs of water—
      could no more be done
         in this mixed company
than to play a tape of Neptune's farts.
      What a divine blessing!
Whales glide up the morning wind
and on a thousand pages of transcript
         modulate her breath
stroking the waves of the lagoon.
           The ancient gods
reach for their daily business,
clamber out of bed
blowing noses between fingers,
         assemble whales
to sing in chorus on the cresting tide
where the sea greets San Ignacio:
      Oh aged prophet,
swallowed by our great fish,
         the fish of Empire,
      turn your glorious voice into light,

kiss the woman's lips below her belt
        with the smell of sliding water,
now lodge your tongue into your birth-place
        and hear your repertoire!
There. Now.
        Is *that* not worth the crossing?

THREE

We didn't include the music.
        An ideal would be
to take the vocables of life
        and weave them to the whales
deaf in the deep
        with their naked language
                perfectly
   misunderstood.
To go in at the ear,
to generate the marvel of that song,
(his back turned to us
as the back of God is,
in the ancient stories,
away from his brother gods
that we be not affrighted,)
              to bear the question
whether to issue at the rear
in a boom of bubbles, oil
        rising to the surface as if all our wells
had blown their tops at once,
             that would have to be
the subject for a grant proposal.
   But we must not make public
this ceremony of the dive.   /   Let me sing to you
   the brackets only.
            (I am going to tape).
   He is singing only the whale songs.
But the whole of creation is in question.
   Or more precisely: all creativity.
      They are fragments

of quite a marvelous poem:
                              mind
          picking out stones
                    in step by step
            transit down stream,
          the hardest work we know:
        same work as following the voice
        rides on another's voice.
And while the whales glide up the morning wind
    all ears are closed.
Mastery towers, however, above all voices.
          Hear them or not:
          Amen. Let it be so.

SIX

What is NOT song?
What will dare
            NOT become song?
Will grass
            refuse to become song?
Will flowers?
                      Will fish
not become song
making a speech in poetry?
(leave us *one* song to ourselves
            they might say
and give us all *your* poetry!)
Will the animals
            not become song?
What will pack-rat do,
red rattlesnake,
fox on the desert's edges:
will they refuse to become song?
      And what will deer do—
will they shy away from song
                and hide among thickets
on the other side of the lagoon?
                      And the whale,

as long as the wall of China,
              will the whale herself
not become song?

SEVEN

How long will it be
before the desert catches fire
and the sea comes home with all its fellow creatures?
Your voice over the hill
as you shape shells into a pattern,
your gray parka beside you,
pointing toward the arctic
gives me an answer,
shaping our common mind,
and takes me back
              to the cool evening we met
and the whole of solitude lay between us.
              But:
how did it happen
that the waters parted and we met?
              Shy. You said. Timid. Shy.
This discussion has gone on far too long
and the rapman has no more to say.
We are moving into an era of meaningless question
       and polite, political answer.
There is hardly anything left to listen to.
                            You hint at me
it is time to recuperate, in enemy discourse,
       each friendly sound.
How forgiving we must yet grow:
       can we really make it?
Unless, of course: No Enemy.
       Meanwhile, sand turns to gold
          as it cascades
              toward the lagoon
                  and breaks against waves.
       Now waves are solid
          and sand flows like water.

Ah, dear god, give us the night out of thy bounty
if thou art bountiful, lower-case god, and if not
let it be the desert of our misunderstanding then,
                        but at least *our* desert.

                (Optional finale:)
            In another moment,
                we may yet meet,
            in another moment,
                we may yet consummate,
                    with just another effort,
                        the canopy may be erected
            and the room be full of sea, sands, pearls,
                waves breaking over our ears
            and whales singing out on mountain tops with birds
                            breathing our air again!

                In another moment,
                        when the sun shines out of the clouds
                    yes, sand will catch fire,
                we shall make speech,
                        we shall meet in the fire.

FROM: NORTH RIM

Singing for you
in the old voice newly returned,
page after page darkens
with the script of your body,
          we are caressed
by a contingency as sharp
          as a whale's watch
(cavorting round the ship
          so it would seem
and for our seeming pleasure):
but I know the whale at his business
in buried kelp
as I know my voice and recognize
we are the only beings in the world
          to satisfy a longing
not even the stars know about
          as the ship starts out again
on her determined journey,
taking all the paths she knows
and weaving them
into the trackless waste we are
          outside ourselves

::

I would write you
into the pages of this sea
if I were captain in some charge
          of my own fate:
but I am like a ship
          without command
and without officers, or destination.
          Turn, woman of
my heart searching for home
      and bring this page to
    unraveled passages
the sea still knows the secret of

and could tell me about
              were I to make you
queen of this northern waste I own:
              as if some part of paradise
unlooked for and unrecognized
              had been assigned
                        worthy of us and of our name

::

                        . . . asleep
                              and
we would come to ourselves in the grass
                        shouting fire
    (as if from a great disaster):
the purple wave
of weed would tumble over
us waking together to the sea—
                        from which
in a froth like the cloud cap at the pole
              a whale breaching
would cross and cross again under the bow
and his mate, when he had sounded, crossing,
then sounding, and he crossing,
              each one each other's shadow—
that fathomless, out of the blazing grass . . .

::

Doors of the sea
        closing behind my incapacity,
              the ship
moving into the ocean
        suspended from three stars
with the sun behind her
        dying in Prince William Sound.
Losing her name,
her passengers and destination,
        surge in the night, going,
and about to be lost.

Interstellar winds
dance with her in far space
our blindness has no conception of—
it has to do with her own lack of title
and purpose at the heart of purpose.
       Morning finds her,
tying her down to schedules
       she'd rather disregard.
              I'm for the night
with all its black disdain of human failure,
   dim details of a coast outside the Sound
where land continues like a broken spine
   willing a body forward though its spirit
has lost all inkling of the sea's direction

::

To have missed a vocation:
       monk of the sea
waking the islands at daybreak
and putting them to sleep
       as the sun
begins his nightly visitation with the dead,
              and further out,
opening and closing the ocean's gates
until the ultimate rim is reached,
              gathering there
all the untethered islands in one flock
       on the black pasture
(where the ice begins)
with their hymns to the sun returning
   and all the marvelous morning
              in my own ears
and in none else . . .

::

Light aura
       around the island
grass on fire

on the high crests,
knives crossed, the walrus
        swaying from side to side
lumbers into the sea,
        more birds than we have ever seen
in our whole lives
        filling the aura with their shadows—
one final day
        life will evidently come to be
this blinding island
                this astonished love

::

We have left the kingdom of ivory:
                        plough south
through the sea's fields toward St. Paul
                and St. Matthew gives us
a last touch of the white in its own bird
        more snow than the snowbird himself,
all white completely,
                except the wingtips dipped
in driftwood charcoal.
                Ink from the sea's own wells
as black as the "lovable Agafon Lestenkov"
whom his father saw clawed down into the dark
                off the bright ice
a century ago it seems to him, at his pulpit,
                counts the faceless sailors
crawling through his church, watches
        out of a window, the bellowing hills
where the seals also go down into the dark
                clubbed to a cloud of blood
out of a louring sky

::

On the high grass
above gentle hills
        and the huge bay studded with islands

of a tropical green
             newly enameled,
    the children of Atka smile
showing all their teeth
    at a moment's relief
from inbreeding.
             I cry metal tears
for all the places
    I shall never see in this life,
clasp you in a passionate embrace
while ravens bell overhead,
             roll back and forth
spinning you round and round
while all the earth spins also
and the green ripples like a skin
             over the iron hills

::

The ship drifts away
from all the continents we know
             into a mapless sea
of uncertain colors —
             but your body remains
anchored among the islands
at the end of this particular earth
             or sits above the weather
like a hawk awake
to any slip or slither in the grass
             my heart might try,
a vole surprised at play,
             when in my ignorance
of where I am, or am likely to be,
(quit of all harbors finally)
I see or sense your smile
             in the round darkness of the void

::

. . . after whole days at sea . . .

The ship was
never still
never silent
and never private.
     Here on Hokkaido
green waves of silence
climb every hill
and there are white birds
         taking wing
between the crispest sheets.
They glide us into havens
where I can touch you sleeping
and leave my hand on your body

::

Light wakes,
an insistence remembered—
     old sea
in the back dunes of childhood.
       Mountains wait,
capes just passing flower.
     Can you find, I ask you,
a central corner for these papers
I shall need later from the suitcase
         but not now?
     That is all, you say,
you have ever wanted, isn't it,
       a central corner
in which to store your life?

::

Black Mountain
       Kurodake,
climb into clouds
billowing ghosts
sensual to the curve of hills,
   quick in their uplift,

210

passionate on the wind.
                    I am old
getting too old for mountains,
heart pounds, too many stops—
                    while you
    stream up the curves
            red fox
through monkshood, foxglove,
                    and high up
(recalling another Black Mountain)
        where the flowers shrink
                    to small blue stars
I suddenly remember the meaning of
        the traveling life,
my face to the lichens
                    in the singing wind

::

The oldest guide in these parts
            speaks of the stately dance
of guillemots on Teuri.
                    Ocean blue women
with long black hair,
            sky beads and gold,
dance as birds in Asahigawa
reminding us of captive cranes
wings far too summer-wet to rise.
                    The oldest
        takes your hands,
speaks to you in a dying language
                    of air and ice,
    sunlight streaming at the sacred window,
the art of growing old gracefully
                    still singing ...

::

Rain swallow,
     ama tsubame,
busy time's scythe
     but far faster
slices the air
     above Teuri:
          black knife
through a grey rainbow
made of delicate cloud.
At the busy hour of birds
          all of a sudden
life is tolerable again,
the birds hone to a sharpness
          our remembering
that we have never traveled before,
          will not travel again,
are not traveling now.

PALENQUE

In memory of Dennis Puleston, taken by lightning,
Chichen Itza, June 1978

"Let the order of ideal time
be asserted and let me
be at the center in the
fire which is still
and does not consume":
an aging man
walking up a steep street,
his mouth on the move
as if he were speaking.
The city he walks is four hundred
and fifty years old—add him
for half a millennium.
It is a place he first came
out of the center to, the first time,
a quarter century ago,
and from here he is going now
to the center again
for the third time.
In the photographs
of the city taken in those days,
there are, even in empty streets,
shadows against walls but no people.
He sees the trees
surrounding Santo Domingo so tall
they are as tall as the trees of
the imagination of his childhood,
as he walks backward in time
with his neck to the future
like a victim. The house walls
of this city are low
but fall still further inward
when entered into,
gardens of inner light
his adolescence loved

where his native country
bathed in her body liquids
at the very center of the earth.
Later: they moved that navel
of earth and sky many times,
his own centers shifted,
taking over every quarter of the globe.
He was an empire, you might have said,
to himself—though a silent one,
little publicized: no cult centers,
no tourist venues. In the gardens,
there are enough lilies to bury all poets,
first and foremost the poet fool enough
to decree that one garden be all white
(the one he lived in)
against the natural miscegenation of colors.
In *his* city, there was to be
no racism, the aging man decreed—
he was tired of all
that reminded him of difference,
the record-keeping of difference,
the separating sessions,
the various faces of time. "Let it all
behave together now and not have me
trying to put salt like a child
on a sparrow's tail" seemed to say
the voice of the man coming upstreet
to the domes with snakes in their hair
and inharmonious bells.
Inside the aging man,
there is a young man running
in all directions at once, trying to reach
at breakneck speed, and simultaneously,
what the older man tries to reach slowly
if he wishes to reach it at all.
The younger man has eyes
full of light and his heart
balances the weight of all he'll give
to that light's source when he meets it.

The young man wakes early
to be the first in a bus line
for distant mountain villages
on fiesta days when they light up the church
like a living heart. He has spent
all night calculating how many
ravishing textiles he can afford
from a store in the Calle Gabriela
the morning after next.
He also has his eye
on a new edition of the *doings of conquest*
which may cost him a meal or two
if he is going to hit every fiesta
and buy every one of those textiles.
The older man wearies fast
with the comings and goings
of the younger man inside him
so that he finds it difficult
to bite exactly on his own aspirations.
"The order of ideal time *may* be approaching,
it is possible poets do *not* have the exact
knowledge of their own life's courses the way I
think they do, from birth to death"
he whispers to himself, coming up hill
toward Comitán 7 where he is staying
without much rhyme or reason.
He has a habit
of landing up more often than he used to
in places unrelated to himself.
"Hill goes up, hill goes down: same street"
he thinks to himself as he enters the house.
It could be explained why he lives on Comitán
this weekend, and it could even be made
interesting in that the wife
of another poet, a famous one,
twice married to him   /   twice divorced, vies there
with sanity, and loses daily.
"I should therefore be doing something
a little more precise than my daily program,

I should be able to make up my mind whether to move
backward or forward from here
if, I mean, backward or forward *signifies*
in a dedicated Life."
"Why," someone had asked him, on the day before
"why, having done something as good, professionally,
as—citing some article in a Textbook—you should
change names, countries, jobs,
leave family and children,
disappear like a thief in the night"
his could-be colleague had asked, then, jumping:
"but you *are* changing courses again now,
that is visible" the colleague said, and our man:
"As to changing courses" (with marked fa-
tigue) "no, merely pushing this course a little,
what is already there, don't you see,
and stressing this a little instead of that,
but, change,
deflecting courses, no, I think not,"
whereupon the could-be colleague,
asked about the politics of land and oil
knew very little about a major airfield to the south
or the size of a related army base—
they were on the wrong scale of analysis.
The only thing our friend could get his teeth into
was that they were destroying in the south
a place he had always felt to be a candidate
for the exact belly-button place;
it was being destroyed with high-rise,
appropriation of Native lands and jobs,
golf clubs, air strips, floating hotels,
condominiums of senior citizens of his own country
and of the country in which the place stood.
"Perhaps" he thought, as he went into his room,
"it would be good to try to save the place"
which was a lake, and stood up inside his memory
every time he thought of it, as if a wall
of water had stood up inside his head,
draining all else.

If there were nothing other to believe in,
at least this could be done for other people's
children, if not his own.
Now, at the evocation
of the lake being saved, the buildings bombed
or otherwise pulled down, against development,
against all likelihood, the volcanoes
going back to their pristine
mirroring of themselves in the lake,
cloud-fingers at dawn unseen by anyone
except the workers in the smoking villages,
another place he had recently come from
rose to his mind, a place he had tried
in his youth to get to, twenty-five years before,
and failed because of empty pockets.
It was the year exactly
the belly of the earth was being opened
and a huge stone, down in the underworld,
gave birth to the city's king,
enabled our scholars to name him,
to have some bite on him,
and out of this was dawning,
even among the driest minds,
(like an emergence from that first earth,
or from a conch shell—the history of music—
or from the smoke in the gods' cigars
when they'd been smoking stars all night)
a confluence of such knowledge, breaks in the code
of such magnitude, that not only this city,
but all the cities round about, the whole empire,
was perhaps about to be understood. And, so many years later,
with a fatter purse, he had at last been able
to go there. "This people" he had thought
as he approached the place
at long long last—
older and older buses,
the place being far
away from anything,
mule trains for days,

a strip in the jungle,
a small plane lifting him
high into rain-cloud,
flying like that for hours
to the limits of fuel,
before leap-frogging a last ridge,
banking sharply over a river,
two macaws flashing,
red, yellow, blue from monotonous trees
under the wings, the pilot, an artist,
putting him down with a whisper in the forest
and the forest closing over him for days.
All around him the trees had risen
much taller than the walls of Comitán,
even taller than the trees around Santo Domingo,
which look now like the tallest on earth,
and, above the trees, palaces had soared
at the top of immense stairways
weeping down into jungle
stone tears through maidenhair
and other exquisite deep plants.
There, he said later to a very few,
he had witnessed events
unrecorded in any history and not
to be put down on paper by anyone
at any time henceforward.
Flying back, in and out of rain,
from the imperial place, he had believed
he might be able to link past and present together
as no one in any discipline seemed able to do.
It would take a heavy investment of time,
perhaps a dozen dialects, he calculated,
and that would keep him occupied for such
remaining days as he had left
—before the reign of ideal time he clamored for—
but it would also be worth doing
for the sake of others' children,
to the outermost children
and limit of mankind, why not: *such* heroism!

He could save a place,
save a culture,
link one culture relevantly with another,
perhaps with all others: many things undreamed of yet
might be possible from here, and
"Why should I know them now, in advance,"
he asked (an old temptation),
moving out of Comitán 7
and about to go into Dr. Navarro 5, the house he had
been asked to sit about a week,
and, from it, you could see the trees of Santo Domingo,
and the garden was drowning in white
lilies everywhere you looked—plus
he had been "given" a bird, for this chosen time,
Mountain Diglossa—"then, why this bird
rather than any other?" he asked himself,
"but it is pleasant,
rather unusual after all, why should I complain:
bluebird colors, sharp beak, long legs,
about 4 inches, works inside fuschia bushes,
and I have never seen it anywhere before."
He passes first the old Native beggar
he passes every day, promising that on the last
day of his stay, or his half century,
whichever would come first,
he would drop into his astonished hat,
the man being blind, a larger note than usual,
"something being accomplished this way at least"
he thought to himself as he found again
the princess he had failed to find in the imperial city,
though all he had met had told him of her
another hundred unrecordable stories:
"Oh the burden of recorded time," he thought,
"how it wearies, how it consumes me,"
(here nearly breaking into Handel as a joke),
"How it keeps me from that home I have always
known the place of, (but lost the key so often,
or deed, or right of entry)—lost to so much
FOOLISHNESS!" he hollered all of a sudden, as

he went through the door, causing a scatter
among the grackles, and the princess laughed, "So
let the order of ideal time" he repeated
"be asserted and let me
be at the center
now without ever leaving it
in the fire which is still and does not consume."

seeing america first

For Janet Rodney

BEFORE THE SNAKE

Sitting, facing the sun, eyes closed. I can hear the sun. I can hear the bird life all around for miles. It flies through us and around us, it takes up all space, as if we were not there, as if we had never interrupted this place. The birds move dioramically through our heads, from ear to ear. What are they doing, singing in this luminous fall. It is marvelous to be so alone, the two of us, in this garden desert. Forgotten, but remembering ourselves as no one will ever remember us. The space between the trees, the bare ground-sand between them, you can see the land's skin which is so much home. We cannot buy or sell this marvelous day. I can hear the sun and, within the sun, the wind which comes out of the world's lungs from immeasurable depth; we catch only a distant echo. Beyond the birds there are persons carrying their names like great weights. Just think: carrying *X* your whole life, or *Y*, or *Z*. Carrying all that *A* and *B* and *C* around with you, having to be *A* all the time, *B*, or *C*. Here you can be the sun, the pine, the bird. You can be the breathing. I can tell you, I think this may be Eden. I think it is.

from: the rectangles

N.B.: The "Rectangles" are not prose poems. They are lyrical poems composed on the typewriter, with each line taking up exactly the same number of spaces. Hence, they merely look like prose by being justified on both sides. Print behaves differently so that the printer's art has been to reproduce the typewriter's effect in print. (This did lead to a few compromises.)

NOR WAS IT POSSIBLE THAT YEAR TO GET AWAY

Friends will break his heart at great length
this summer, "an eminently breakable heart,"
by leaving these hills and valleys behind to
fly through the windows of several memories:
one toward beaches lit by flowers and flags
against the paradisal blue of a northern sea
(and where should *he* get that childhood blue
again—if north in paradise does not exist),
another into mountains drilling sky for hail
over the furthest ranges of a shuttered west
and a third will go into the eternal cities,
refreshing himself only with light on stone.
Under the parasol in Monet's Sainte-Addresse
whispers every secret of an invisible world:
ten thousand things he has still not sighted
never weigh lighter for his aging shoulders.
Yet mapled here the kingbirds black on white
scat a little taller each time when the heat
lifts lead one day in ten from summer's head.

"THE SELECTION OF HEAVEN"

I. M. Paul Blackburn

Almost as if love . . . listen: bird / bird,
high in the highest tree, were to remind him,
as if bird hid in the same place as his mind,
re-reading Paul's consignment of John Henry—
granddaddy from his grave of earth, his dying
to the ivy-green, sea grave of Walter's book,
each letter etched and rampant, tick in skin,
today's specific done, done, now carried over
into this other life—how he would collapse,
if he could, everyone of these notions, brand
each into a jewel only volcanos could produce
hurling them out for the invisible companion,
ghost of a distant star, which has not heard,
or only barely, of America. And in these find
the time's trajectory, the "Spirit" billowing
from Golden Gate to Gander in a single flight
to put these travels to rest at last, assuage
Paul, the ceaseless memory of a dying tongue,
worse: warily exploring the silent tongue
that wouldn't titillate again, could spare no
coil: had been so cool at insult, over noise,
so much a ceremonial magus in his music city.

AN IMMIGRANT'S ADDRESS

In the cool of morning, between garbage trucks
and rising slow to coffee and a couple of eggs
on ham and cheese: no toast, no jelly, keeping
the fats away, if the sky be not too contrary,
if they know what the desk will call for sure,
that much security afforded, then: some peace,
some listening to the careful birds pick apart
auspices of day. "This is possibly happiness!"
asserted one bird—he is sure of it—echoing
a proposition he had once inquiringly advanced
"and when we leave here, looking back over it,
who knows if we will not have lived paradise?"
Certainly, the photographs of his May mornings
with their Giverny greens (for Monet'd painted
both Giverny and Pennsylvania) add Likelihood.
They go to air the long black dog which before
its tail, riots along the banks, raising duck.
We both go this morning! they decide for Eden.
The Eden before this one, before all gardens—
frets at their minds unvoiced but unforgotten.

HIS EYES LOOKING FORWARD
AND UPWARD

Meditating "My Brilliant Career" on early walk:
houseful of parakeets protected from pollution,
dusts, hungers of the world, shines in the mind
against a lie of Australasian light. How lovely
the labors of a literature! He looks downwater:
does she follow, the paradisal shadow—and al-
most, almost, o she is found, she is found, she
isn't lost he lifts into himself the filial cry
at the sight of white flox sudden tall as bride
standing on memory. But it is not her—rather,
he sees she is inside him, in his heart's eyes,
in the thirty-three eyes of his spine, burrowed
deeper than she has ever been in Hades. He's in
mid-literature going voiceless it seems to him,
into uncertain futures. Gazing down at the dog,
envying simple frenzies against bone, rat, cat,
remembering the model ship by the desk, pointed
forward. How fast the ship moving with the desk
so long! Time battle-colors go back on the aged
Dodge, twice over to Alaska, once to Guatemala,
now aiming at Quebec. *Nadie me quita lo andado!*

REACHING FOR HÖLDERLIN

Remembering: not to remember that we die, brink
of purest joy at drawing breath in this garden,
with any human smile, before winter comes down,
we who are here such a short season among roses
to be spending time say all day in Pennsylvania,
whose profession is dying—who are so occupied
with time before our time here, and time after,
while fall infects us like a blood transfusion,
(pneuma flown like a sail, heart about to teem:
philosopher in his bath last week, aorta blown)
yet in life's *favor* tell: Professor Von Europe,
Von Mittelerde, smug among dollars and flowers,
tell him of the diaphanous, desired, aura light
surrounding the life of the poet he can't read,
possessing not a single *umlaut* of the language,
(cannot, cannot, looks in the questioning eyes)
and he cannot throw back onto himself his ownly
light aura—as he breaks to where everyone is.

OPENING OUT A LINE
OF MANDELSTAM'S

In that blessed weariness where he's achieved
the best he can with you world, falling apart
as he conjoins, conjoining as he falls apart,
not once the two coming together: in concord,
amity, that synthesis from which they'd sworn
everything flourishes—but now what is this?
—on the edge of the worker's sleep usually—
when he has spent a rare full day at laboring
sensing, secret, mysterious, that recompense:
to feel the whole weight of oneself as a man!
Birds in foliage, inside forest, like a cage,
forest inside the galaxy, like a cage, galaxy
in the arms of someone you would call goddess
were you not so sure you'd seen her someplace
almost recently, had you no reason to believe
you might have desired her once a while back,
or been in debt to her for the warmest friendship
of the most comforting kind: and, around you,
all pleasure, sound of birds, beyond earshot,
guessed at only, as if by her deaf composer—
inexplicable mirth, *joie de vivre* his friends
disbelieve and find it hard to credit you for
with the centuries surrounding you like fire!

OF A MARRIAGE MADE WITHIN
THE GREAT LIGHT

There was so great a noise and—all of a sudden,
silence. Frozen gold sunk down to the pool floor.
Light sunk to the day's floor and, some evenings,
a suggestion of the night not more, shining a bit
behind the sky. On the frozen river, a goose pool
opening at last, a long lead, not comfortable now
but like a gash, a wound on the body of the river
wrapped in her silver shroud. From the silver sky
dusk empties itself of geese: they fly high today
as if permitted closer to the light they venerate
and pass several times to and fro before dropping
in long, low falls to the water. Congress. Noise.
So much conversation. The sum of which is silence
he understands. "How close, how far, *are* you then
from reality today?" she asks. —"Having a superb
passage of time vis-à-vis reality nowadays." Like
an omen of a dread unity underlying all he feels:
in her dress of snow, corpse, bride, who can say.

EYES WATCHING UPSKY

"If you move down into sleep profoundly enough death discovers you and takes you to a violent festival where you give up your name. There is no way you can back yourself up into the world of glorious light. Perhaps you forget you have ever been in that world, yes perhaps you do... the whole gentle motion of living is something you abandon behind you as if it had never been performed. The other night," he says, "I awoke in a sweat inside the chocolate box insulation shanty with the silver foil rustling around me and my eyes faced a field of stars so profound and wide across the belt of the sky, I thought the dead were looking down at me again, out of New Mexico, the deep balconies they keep upsky where they watch us as from behind glass above the floor of our dancing and our transactions, gentle as the insanes'—perhaps far more so."

THE LAST GRAND RAIN

Cézanne, (Monet)

"This land of my desire, that I want, this once,
this of my heart," hand almost on his chest left
in the grand gesture of the grand days they were
reviving now, a peach in wine, swilling memories
of old defeats dissolving into torrents of tears
brought half Provence around bearing consolation
and a wooden toy. "If it weren't for the contour
of this land I love, I wouldn't be here" he owns
now to a toy-maker. "At last they learn from me,
I can teach these forms—which are color only."
In that garden, long ago, with which his brother
had compassed Eden round himself, tamed success,
assembling friends and beginning a long address:
"I am happy—happy to have us all here at last,
so that we can tell you, all together—how very
grandly we affect you and admire you . . ." But he,
numbed, with a rough "You too make light of me!"
grabs hat, swivels, departs. "I have this land,"
he continues to think, "with a mountain at
heart I go on prowling around all the days of my life,
desert tints, small cabins my eyes, old crippled
men: a muse, a wife. Go, send for paint, prop me
against the wall. Bring on the last grand rain."

WITH MY OWN WILL, PHENOMENA
THAT ARE NEW

If, on every desk top, it is necessary that there be a ship, notice: the ship travels insofar as the desk . . . but the desk doesn't move. No more than they'll move, in "The Adoration of the Magi": twin manikin figures, in the far, entering those trees, one clad vermilion, with a white headdress, one green, turned toward her, deep conversation enfolding them, leaving behind them on the yellow field five merry dancers in their solitude. The verdant forest will devour them which never falls victim to the gold she saw this day as the year turned on its side in sleep and the first sign of joy at this long rest to come brushed a whole sun against each and every tree. "That some such days" she'd said that afternoon "be so precious, have so much to give, and with such ease at that—such . . . ahh," exhaling— "whereas all others batter us for breath and shred us merciless: raining neglect, harrow or silence, if not the downright hatred of the massive man." She stayed. Unspeaking words she had never framed, moved backward into the grief of the past: where she opened, opened, unveiled her mouth like a heart and writing answered.

He is no longer called into the eyes of the world,
the streets are no longer a beckoning. He traipses
the mother-city's avenues meditating more and more
on his birth—and it is as if he is safe suddenly
from beckoning. "Did you think in our prison Life,
you would see anything but suffering?"—A. Artaud.
He fancied his body was shining so that no eclipse
henceforth would ever interrupt that bracing light
coming from him in the night dark, or in the day—
it did not matter: for walls were not the answer—
he had to shine above and beyond all light. He saw
no question either, as if all the eyes in the city
had faded from their questions. Long ago, she came
into his life, looking at his face, sans calling—
there is no beckoning if you reckon right. He nods
but does not propose, nor she—they come together
as if planted at the same time in different soils.
"Why do you not answer?" she asks and smiles. "Be-
cause you have never called," he answers and leans
into her eyes and buries his smile in her furrows.
She ploughs her diplomacy through his life's fields—
he reaps a harvest of contentment all their days.

from: the narratives

NARRATIVE OF THE METAMORPHOSIS
OF SPIDER INTO CRAB

In Memoriam: Kenneth Rexroth

As we were choosing a watercolor among those
set out on a table for our inspection
I looked up at the ceiling, white on white,
seeing a spider move at right angles to us
toward a point where she would stand above
the apex of our heads. She was a thick-bodied,
thick-legged, muscular thing, a jumper
of a kind familiar in these parts
(much larger though than any seen before)
with a clown's dress: jet black, white-striped.
Others did not look up and never saw her.
She moved with nice deliberation, stopping
now and again in hesitation, almost as if
she were turning back—but the whole passage
revealed on ending its unerring purpose. Poised
overhead—small doubts perceptible
to the practiced eye: as if there were to be
a retractation or a slip sideways—and the fork
would translate into movement, a circle traced
whose obvious perfection would oppose, in all
its clarity, the doubt apparent in her.
The movements were not entirely spider-like
but rather, in their tentative, backing and
forwarding, scissoring motions a little similar
to scorpions—except I knew this creature far
neater than the scorpion and never treacherous.
And, sometimes, the sideways, almost glancing move
would, with the body's thickness, remind me of
the crab that I inherit. I saw for a moment,

in fantasy, a miniature black cancer move across
a beach rimmed with a turquoise sea,
taking me with her into those possessions
the sand under the sea seals daily in my country.
And, also, it was as if she moved like an eclipsed
shadow over the paintings on the sand-tinted table,
and seemed to turn most hesitant over the one
I finally selected. And all this time, the others,
(I worried specially about my daughter's nerves,
she being fearful of such beasts as much as I:
what if she should catch up the black progression
halted over her head!), did *not* look up, proceeded
with their choices as if those wild decisions
had never crossed their path or intersected with
their fate or interfered in any way whatever
with taste at judgment on the art surveyed.
At the point when, never in haste, the spider
stood to and rested, crouched a fraction,
almost as if for one of her famous jumps,
I felt election move inside my will, small doors
open and close in the brain, the eye acute,
secure in all its shutterings — and, there and then,
as if under an influence, made my final choice
among the paintings: which one would hold which wall
for the duration of my life. Above the ceiling,
topping the roof, uncounted miles into the sky, beyond
all boundaries attained by any human effort,
within another life (as it was said of us, moving to this
absolute desert of the mind: "as for the sky here,
mind you, it is another country — pure, perfumed,
tender to skins, delicious as a draught
of juices from the crop of all the fruits of summer")
there stood, I'm sure of it,
one vast, spread-eagled cancer with its claws awake,
radiating light, in talk with other beasts,
their huge extremities also emitting light,
watching on member populations here below —
and maybe other planets hidden in the abyss.
Meantime, the spider, on her longitude,
went forward after I had made my own

unmoved, unmoving last determination and from that time,
as we prepared to leave, taking our prize with us,
she used the interval to reach the eastern orbit,
passing the length of the remaining ceiling
to the other shore. There she hid awhile
across a beam as dark as she was: which annulled
her features altogether, except for the white stripes
that almost glowed on the surrounding dark. And,
finally, moving along the beam, she reached a door,
the back door to the house. By then it had been dark
for a few minutes and I hardly saw her moving out
as if drawn on by some invisible machine
pulling her back with all the other stars
into the sky's uttermost asylums.
Here it is she turns, companion to the day's
vast cancer of bright light dating my life.
I will tell you now: there are two skies, not one.
One is the sky of light, huge father to the day.
One is the shadow sky, mother of night.
The sun passes from one into the other on its rounds,
a man at times, at others, a woman. Perhaps you did not
know that. The sun is at his business in the sky,
works on his own behalf along a line of purpose
we know nothing of. At night, he passes
through us, or shall we say: she passes,
and we know all of it. Only sham not to.
What we ignore of what we know makes menacing shadow.
In truth she is our friend, we must not fear her.
Everything we do is locked into her loving aegis.
Whether she passes through our sight or leaves us blind
on that long shore under the sea, battered by tides,
the weather of our worlds, she's like a ship
who, though she's not been warned, has reached her anchorage.

NARRATIVE OF THE MEN AND WOMEN
WHO BECAME STARS

In Memoriam: William Everson

First looked in November, trusted hearsay
for the cold about us made our eyes water
and our ears buzz: *that* blur,
that minute seed, way up among the Pleiades,
might be our object. Soon reached March
and, following instruction in the newspapers,
witnessed, just before dawn, the star distinctly
within its trailing hair, low, unmistakable.
But the brightest viewing would come in April. And here
is mystery: got up, often, at the right hour,
in fact, at a variety of times to saturate the chance,
climbed backside of the house up our steep hill
and stood—a little like a prophet tempted
by worlds about my head in utter clarity. There,
above the Sangres, the object *should* have been—but
was not. After a bunch of days, with clouds to boot
making the sky at best a chancy business, wavered.
And here, nothing had differed much from most
of life: in that the chosen, worked for long and hard,
has, taken all in all and for the most part, failed
to make its due appearance. When self is, then other is;
when self is not, there is no other. And the great way
pours its beneficent milk out of star clusters,
out of broad avenues in the sky's center
which divide the generous breast from the sterile pap.
The great way is silent and impassive, among the galaxies,
completely surrounded by motion in all things but itself still.
We rise every morning, and for twenty-four hours inclusive
shift things around from one place to another.
Initiate transformations which will end up by coaxing
a thing out of its spot into another. Our law is
change—not the stars' change as they move along
the measureless axis dividing all known things,
but the small change we pick out of will's pockets

and slide into the hungry slots of human life.
And from this lours all our misery.
Thinking back: it *is* possible, this
stillness—not to move when the world does not,
not to act when action does not fire of itself
like bird off branch, in flight before it springs,
but has to be extracted, laboriously, out of our brains
as if to stage a sacrifice for bitter gods? That
very republic, discussed so often, is, in essence,
the Republic of calm in which love naturally flowers
at the end of an immeasurable cultivation: the plant,
sculpted out of its roots in darkness, nurtured,
through all its foliations, colorful explosions,
then, unfolding upward into the sky, becoming a star.
It is also Republic of all republics, everywhere, always,
in that everything happens there at the same instant—
we're all alive together, or dead in her, exactly.
Think what it would mean to be the god of such a system
and to have all of that, millennially, alpha to omega,
inside one's belly—quiet, pregnant, pacific,
motionless like the great ocean that we do not see
bathing the stars but governs all our actions primordially
among the pulls and tractions of the universe. Therefore,
it is possible, it may be—that we do not have to mourn
those we have lost in attempting apartments in space,
who were blown into fire like molten glass,
flowers of fire, high above ocean one hopeful morning,
and all through faults in love, in listening attention.
Because in any event they would have become stars in dying
at any time that their death was naturally decreed
(in the sense of a fruit, mature, falling off the bough).
But we, in our pride, had to put them there, to give them
names among the moons of a ferocious planet, instead of
letting them find their settled ordinations among stars.
(But it would have been hard on us, given "national honor,"
to let them do that by themselves, for the good reason
that we'd have had no record: would not have known
their true location, where to look for them in the sky,
at the right or wrong time, where to write them down
in the books of remembrance, as befits "the heroes

of the greatest nation.") Alas, the quiet Republic is no nation,
divided against other nations, at constant war, whether
for now or in some future endlessly predicted,
but a completeness beyond our understanding which is
peace. Let the mind then not rage, not stammer
with violent disappointment at the phenomena unseen—
enough the star has passed, woven its passage through
the lovers' lanes of the great way—enough it has
inscribed itself in history—having arrived,
having gone out on such and such a day. Do we not know
that history is platitude, *la grande misère du tout*,
that the star is always passing, its passages forever
within the scope of record—and that, at any moment,
we can look up at the sky and find them inscribed there,
lodged deep within the mirrors of the divine imagination?

the mothers of matagalpa

In Memoriam: Pablo Neruda

Like the freedom of madmen and the insane:
so that there be no thing on earth or elsewhere
                              cannot be said (by us)
insofar exactly as it won't be listened to exactly—
        a deafness
beyond the proverb CAST NOT PEARLS BEFORE SWINE,
                              & easier for a camel through
            the needle's eye
THAN FOR A DEAF MAN TO ENTERTAIN HEAVEN. So go to:

them, entering long hall, sitting down quietly,
face to face with us, sitting down quietly,
            the long sea flowing in the midst,
now speak most simply, enunciating:
            name, age,
            manner of death,
            place of death,
                    relation-ship in love
            down the middle sea,
                    where death began.

SO THAT simple speech versing into song through,
choral simplicity of it, lacking all decoration.
Leader suggesting, suggesting no more, approach:
all ye closer to one another—ye seeking peace.
Them, as to cue, getting up, smoothing eyes, up.
                              appro-
        aching us.

Us, dropping all our sophistication behind us
    on the seat we leave, (approaching us:)
    this difficult, timid, meandering melt
    of middle earth, still human in dimension—then

us, over-tall, -fat, -stocky, children of
　　our colossal empire, much more great than death,
　　owning it all, giving it down to neighbors,
　　all sundry people, over all earth, starting to
stray to stars now presently, taking death also.

　　As if: there were *madres sin hijos,*
　　(they are mothers without sons),
　　como si, there were children without mothers,
　　　　　　　　　each looking for the other,
from a long time before, aching,

emotion beginning to rise, unfamiliar to us minds,
somewhat filling the throat as if we had swallowed another
body than ours and it were falling down our throats, to the
lungs, belly, gut, womb-filling, placental, coming out in
blood between legs as we struggle to:　　mingle to:
　　　　and the soul
　　　　swimming alone too naked the vast sea,
　　　　　　　　　　　seen gone over ice alone—north,
　　　　　　　　　　　　　further north,
　　　　than anyone outside the empire can imagine.

Madres
not of "heroes and martyrs" like they say
　　but simply children, sons, dragged up through years
into some sort of manhood, early here, singing,
　　　　　　　　　　lyric, rhetoric, analytical,
　　　　just with the chords of the voice
　　　　　　　　　　　like the one (a month gone by,
　　　　flowers purchased just this morning on the way down here)
　　　　　having taken the left eye out,
　　　　　cutting the jugular to let the blood free,
　　　　　barking that will let the communism out of you,
taking out the back brain—gray spill, gray floor,
turning to mud blood (brown here, out of earth)
(not forgetting the ritual castration), (not) (anything)
(forgetting) to (drain) the mother (sea)

HOW IS IT THAT YOUR PRE-ZI-DENT, with so many teeth,
on his gigantic throne, in all that north,
fears us so much a pimple on the map, so much IN-VI-SI-BLE?
How can he, but for insanity, snakes in the mind,
versing the mind to it, changing maybe the composition of
the very d.n.a. of under-standing?   GO NOW: Act! Act!
                    TELL IT LIKE IT IS:
insofar exactly as it won't be listened to exactly—
    deafness to those who think they own
                            the UNI-VERSE, the HEMI-SPHERE,
the LAND-GAUGE: song sung by mother so much long ago, so go,
how could we not but know [CERTAINLY, STILL WITHIN WARRANTY,
NO QUESTIONS ASKED] the way it is, for us, so *there* for them—
in one linguistic god, one lyric, even this structured dog
                    between one mother's legs, latent,
that brine of pain, feels empire on his eyes, closes, dozes,
                    intelligence asleep to cut from this.

And then the question arises,
as it does among some women, fallen to spasms in one corner,
the whole PACIFIC of it, washed over them again,
    "how do we *do* this? how *can* we do this?"
    —which, upon questioning reveals
that this is done twice or thrice *a week*
                            in "slack times"
but twice or thrice *a day*
                    when times are "busy"—
    the country near-dead now of delegationitis—
examined right down to the asshole time over time, to
check if this, permissible, that, permissible, so we can be
COMFORTABLE with this/that, on our high throne up north,
while the buck goes down, going on down, so we can be
COMFORTABLE at this level, low-intensity level, invisibility war . . .

                            So that this dance,
and song, is *not* spontaneous, *not* fit to make the heart
leap up into the mouth for song, as the con-vention goes,

as in-spiration falls, but, while it looks that way, dis-
tances you [Bertolt B.], epic, stopping you, tracks, anal-
yzing you, breaths, repro-ducing you [Walter B.], inform-
acting you (coming to the margin), makes it worth your while,
(coming to the point of sitting this one out) falls to fight
another day, onwordily however:
   as a critique of the discourse of power,
   muriéndome un lunes, un martes, un miercoles qualquiera,
   (sintiéndome un poco lunes al empezar)
               aber freund! wir kommen zu spät!
   without alternative
              to recover the meaning of words?

but, at least, that we do not fight among ourselves,
using up all that precious energy (*zu spät*)
there being out there all that LABOR,
   m'en allant défendre MA *révolution(g)*
          in all these sounds of the free ocean:

Two hours north + or − exactly, into the war zone,
but with mothers all over the place, in every city,
village, co-op, who should forbid their thighs perhaps,
as the old poet had it:
          until they die of.

   AQUÍ NO ONE SURRENDERS
   NO ONE SURRENDERS HERE
   AQUÍ NO SE RINDE NADIE.
                 until we die of. And we do.
                 And we do:

it being better to be a fluke in the gut of a sheep
than a poet drowned by chance in the ocean of this *imperium*
   that called itself, once proudly, a REPUBLIC
         (hail perishing)
         "and was to be the smile of all the world":

TRASHED, WASTED, DAMN NEAR GONE
                    in mind-rot. Imbecility. Inertia
    of the soul

swimming alone too naked the vast sea
asking what will become of us—who should have been

[and the story will be told (later) how left *or* right,
we require the *land*, and will kill *all* to get it,]

such friends, kissing those mothers' cheeks—fall into action,

as if—meaning the real of it.

flying the body

In Memoriam: Muriel Rukeyser

ONE

Alpine, we start from sky:
      thrust of elation, (drag of terror
that we be held below
      by hands of darkness)
into a lift of light
      at play over the mountains:
so life might be translated to
      light and light's gaiety
for moments we are given in free air.
      Imagination grasps the whole:
sky lore identical in song.
      Death down the only difference—
satanic interruption—
      and the return to land
of this heavy body
      just a passing sleep
until the next day's somersault
      of heart and mind
into such hospitable height.

THREE

Ever earth's envy of liberating us,
        no more assuming hold on us,
or, ever-loving, unwilling to fall back
        into oblivion as we cruise above—
and constantly, like a desire in mind
        not quite forgotten, calling us down
into its hands again. Jealous to death:
        because down may be terror
if spinning out of cruise
        arms out and passionate,
(holding up body),
        but both arms stalled and so on down
into earth's jealousy—
        unless the mind will hold, reason hold,
arms level out of sickness,
        into anticipated health—to sail again
at fathering height. But jealous mothers
        accept no closured signals,
holding a child down by the feet,
        hands gripped round ankles.
No, life is not your mother say the instruments:
        death in its darkness is—all that safety
you think is yours below disguises traps
        you may fall prey to daily, while above
a fair illusion holds, smiling cloudless.

FOUR

In sky always a fear
      the trap will open:
the flimsy doors,
      or worse the floor, fall through,
not to the ground
      (that factual enough)
but to a deeper landscape
      where jealous earth
waits with cold hands
      (her servants warning her
of those in peril)
      to snuff us out.
Wisdom declares
      not even in free falls
are you for one fell moment
      losing in any sense—
and yet how not to ask:
      between death's fingers
is there one breath or not
      to take before the burn,
before all difference fades
      and the same path opens again
we've always flown
      as long as memory.

SEVEN

Time has crept up on you—
        deceitful travel season—
summer falling behind, winter advances.
        And this small changing of the guard
among all clocks sweeps you later to air
        by half the morning.
You hardly notice it
        as first maneuvers keep you abreast
of the horizon—and you shift yourself
        into the false pride of control.
"No it is not this frame I fly
        but I myself I pound through air
with this peculiar soughing
        in my ears!" Then waking wind
which has been skulking in the mountains
        outs and throws punches at you
left, right, now underneath—
        and though you reassert direction
yet shakes an attitude you thought attained
        in most cool patterns of achievement.
This enemy you cannot see rams pride
        back to its sockets. Ghost eyes look out
along the chain of mountains, searching there
        for the wind's hide-out: so you might know
where he will come from, tipping you over—
        but it won't ever be revealed too clearly
to lend you any permanent approaches
        or solve the finals of this riddling world.

TEN

Weather has held you down
      until you totally believed
all was forgotten. But now,
      with a long rest, what you had thought
unmemorizable moves into hands and feet.
      It is not you holding up the height,
eyes glued to watches, scared
      of moving millimeters from the true,
but arms, now swimming of themselves,
      as if they had decided to be wings,
flesh breasting air at slightest touch —
      with time to consummate this roll
or that leveling out — and even leisure
      to make tomfool mistakes, leap-frog
beyond the point where you should touch
      this earth again. Some particles of
mastery moved in your blood, some secret
      synapse passed a message on,
as yet barely deciphered, could make you shift
      this weight through sky one day
as if by instinct. A length of time
      (because no guarantee can come of this
for the next effort) yet shyness lost
      as if sheer weight were now another dancer
you helped to lift, sweep through the air,
      her body coming closer, you undismayed,
or not as much as you were shown to be
      when she set eyes on you, in the beginning.

TWELVE

In case there is no control
      to tell you where to move the body
and bring it back to land
      from its dreamtime up there,
it is better to speak to no one
      than not to speak to someone
(should a someone be about
      both of you dangerous
to each, and all the bodies else
      milling around this sky).
Which is why there are rules
      of infinite complexity
to govern this vast silence
      and how to break it
on entering its various domains,
      pockets of stringent safety,
no eye discerns, both ears at bay alone
      to shape the emptiness
into a formal menace.
      It can be nightmare:
those other bodies minuscule most times
      suddenly huge without transition:
appalling tangle, beaks and wings,
      crisscross of arms and legs,
the fall, all waxes melting.

FIFTEEN

Held as if wombed and tombed all this long time,
          as if a victim to some sacrifice
on a round altar—that is the path imprinted
          from up to down all through these weeks
bending the body to its will to fly—
          but not all flight takes the imagination!
When do you gain the liberation
          all dwell on lovingly who have achieved it?
And then, one day, there is no down just yet
          but out and off beyond the crucible:
sky suddenly grown tall, averse to measure
          exact parameters gripped you before.
Here is the world revealed, body's home
          now infinitely small under the belly,
so small you cannot tell down there
          who drives south to a town, east to a city,
and all particulars fade out below the sun.
          Anxious, eye scans the sky for joy:
where is that joy which once was promised you?
          Freedom you should have had up here
now that the body leaps at liberation?
          Sun homing to this heart from death
in western mountains all these latter years?
          And you imagine and connect with image:
that you do what you seem to do—as a free agent?

SEVENTEEN

When you are not (up and around)
        in sky then you are sleeping:
sky takes it out on body
        in the most fearsome way.
And when you are not sleeping,
        a snow may fall so white
it is impossible to witness to the blue—
        what, under ideal circumstance,
the body likes to fly so it can dream.
        That sense of shutting out
is like release, a comfort, and, as well,
        at the same time, a punishment
as if you were excluded
        from havens of desire. Few remain.
Remember now what he said yesterday
        how once again to bring the body down:
what rushes back beneath you is already past,
        what moves ahead of you cannot be reached.
What stays immobile—like sun among the planets—
        is where you may yet ground this life again.

poems 1985–1998

BREUGHEL AT WIEN

For Jerome Rothenberg

Our lives are led before us,
      before we lead them—
      or are we *there*?
Are our days inside us
      lived fully, without escape?
Or is there always a little door
      in the background
            through which they drain away?
      Saul transfixed by his sword,
a thousand pikes crossing him out below.
      Paul surrounded with pines
(consistency of feathers),
      erased by mountains,
falling toward Damascus—his afterlife
      come down upon him
invisible to the vast army locks him in.
      Casual butchery
of Jerusalem children,
      snow falls on innocence,
crystals melt in blood.
      World taking place in a crucifixion:
(*no:* the earth does *not* turn!)
      and a cross crown
pierces our heaven right enough
      through the sun's eyes—
bearing another citizen to birth
      in a virgin's lap.
Godhead losing itself out of the world:
            armies on horse sauntering by,
crows spying cripples from the clouds,
      far wheels of people circling Golgotha.
        Then there is Babel rising
    as it did in the beginning
      turning to Babylon
    which has not ended yet

(and never will—)
            so much does beauty need,
      require this multitude of tongues
          (and sufferings)
to voice her favored art
            and give the palm to hope.

::

The childhood gone:
      small blonde girl
      bouncing in the night
in a pink gown
      with laughing eyes
      and laughing body,
moving everywhere
      with a dancer's grace
      (can only be lost?)
Questioning eyes:
          Why are the innocents dead?
Why did they not eat their food today?
      Why did father not play with me:
        always alone
and occupied beyond the call of reason
      over all my prayers?
Child gone now
      into the corridor—
darkness beats like a heart
        in some forgotten body.
      Innocents stifled,
a massacre: silk and blood veils
      as quiet as the wind has grown
over our country.
           And my eyes have died
that could see all the world
      with piercing freshness
yet lacked a mirror at their core
      to throw back to her eyes
the only truth would bury solitude
      in the cave of love.

::

I live among the foolish
who have no innocence at all
        and hence no wisdom.
I have lost the child forever
        who once had prophesied it
one night so long ago:
                I used to mourn in the night
        waking in storms of fear
and seeing nothing beyond the white
        shifts of the curtain's whispers.
In the child, the parent lost
who had lost his life down the generations
                        to the uttermost sin.
Startled, black-eyed,
        stare into darkness,
the sockets empty, eyes rotted,
where dark sees dark, knowing only the dark's
        murdering comfort.

::

Almost as if the children came
        out of another world
they had not lived in childhood:
                though saw them there,
but before this birth
                in some other eden
covered with snow
                by blackbirds overflown.
From which there would erupt
the pleasures of baked bread,
soup slurped at common tables,
thick peasant hands eager to clasp
their heavy womens' hands and leap around
        to the bagpipe's music . . .
                and dance into creation,
a holy family,
                back out of birth and death
                        into their paradise.

SEGALEN (VICTOR) TRAVELS WITH GAUGUIN (PAUL); ENCHANTED BOTH: LATER AT NUNUE

For Lindsay Hill

"Je pouvais dans mon sommeil m'imaginer l'espace
au dessus de ma tête" ("le grand toit élevé de feuilles
de pandanus"), "la voute céleste, aucune prison où
on étouffe—Ma case c'était l'Espace la Liberté"

—NOA NOA

Cloud forehead into which we glide,
blue lower lip juts into sea,
island nose advanced, gigantic prow,
landing onto lip's surface like a kiss—
feathering props, welcoming palms—
in a movement of wind will never cease
as long as our hands hold up mountains.
Island wilting in moist air,
storm gathering around entire horizon,
impossible to know from exactly where
but everything trembles in the three creations.

::

All night above our heads waiting to sleep
scratching and scrawking of sooty terns
among high palms (from the cosmic standpoint
what *is* the question of the other species?
How do they think this world into becoming:
with us—or else without us?)
Afterward, sleep in sea arms
covered by her deep blue shoulders
shielding us from incendiary stars—
"all that gold and sun rejoicing" you said—
ferocious as our household planets.

::

Girl with smile wide as world
you have taken to wife,
inside whose sky invested fathers dream,
painted by you as where are we becoming,
whose acquiescing arms turn into sea,
whose children curl where tuna sleep
safe from shark tooth and tail,
remembers ships like trees on the horizon.
"Blind they came from behind our sky:
strangers with grasping hands outstretched;
their own sky void, children starving,
so powerful their famine to be eating us;
paddles silent, probably cloth-wrapped,
invisible along the mountains' sides:
who ride high ocean on heavenly sails,
who come inside a man by stealth and his head
is lost in an instant as you are dreaming
and there is no longer creation-sky—
his frame hurled lances with such precision
stone now with neither head nor voice—
and there is no longer creation-earth
smothered in bleeding surf."

::

The people cry tonight, their eyes
inside their heads—"Save us! Save us!
it is evening, it is evening of the gods!"
mourning great islands wrapped in golden mist
never to be recovered. Three stars tonight,
rest devoured by cloud. Men walk the reef—
whole air made god of this astounding light,
all voyage stilled, birds sky-suspended,
(spirits in ancient pictures visiting home)
even fish in deep pools no longer flying
above their dead—universe suspended
in a beyonding louder than silence
whose song again would bear significance
(surf howling far, conch blast, prayer surge):
"Oh paradise-eve on treasury of waters

when will our freedom swell from this oppression,
when can we glide our flocks again
over satin lagoons, across unheard of islands! . . ."

::

Weave of terns above velvet water
writing in air paths fish may take
stalking their victims in anxious circles,
startle our eve with peevish cry
against a fate withholding sustenance.
People arrayed at sunset over beach
wide as the universal shore and just as pale
awaiting miracles—birds in dark contrast,
sooty even at dusk, flying patrols
warning assemblies that this cannot happen.
Yet this great ship of *our* dread empire
sings in her wind against the people,
all sails deployed, ready to leave
and not a man on board with any heart
might hurt throughout this darkness,
no officer nor captain—all enterprise
vast, empty and at terror over any ocean,
winging for capital into harm's way.

::

Sea closes over eyes, eyes become sky:
through sky descend translucent fish
softened by sea lips, water so generous,
a warmth outpouring oil of hydromel,
fish may begin immediately we enter—
so scarcely visible we do not see them
until our feet pass through their ranks
last of creations, creation-water,
until we are on top of them,
gliding past one way at eye level
trailing our dream before reversing.

::

As if all men were now to drown in ocean,
all ocean life to beach, begin a breath.

MINIATURES, RAJASTHAN/PUNJAB HILLS, 1990

N.B.: These are not translations but poems inspired by Indian miniature paintings. Names after titles (except the last, a poet) signify schools of painting.

For N.J.M.

Plane Tree with Squirrels, Mughal

Plane tree bears a whole sky of leaves
Gold leaves in conversation with silver stars
Poised squirrel constellations, tail stops and commas
To the huge poem of the universe unfolding
Birds dart between lines and branches
Hushed hunter lifting foot, breaks into paradise

Megh Mallar Raga, South Rajasthan

Skies dark with promise open in your picture
Cloud music plays, peacocks thirst for rain
Great tails lift in a cloud of liquid sunshine
Beaks quiver toward cloud—it seems a century
Since our bodies united, trees reach for sky
Blossoms point up, rains down over us together

Lady at Tryst, Bundi

Concentration of garden in the sun's womb
Riot of flowers and birds englobes you
Candle in a blue dress, taut arrow-wary doe
Garlands enhance the door, point to it, how many
Flowers to work through till I pierce this hide
And all creation can begin to dance around us

Lovers Hunt at Night, Peripheral Basohli

Riding the wind at night on fast round horses
Looking into each other's eyes, never losing them
Thus can attend to the world, stalk an animal
Bring down a bird, finish an enemy, rescue a friend
And yet hold fast to unwavering center—but eyes
Are two by two, no wonder love breeds a third

Blue God Summons Cows, Bilaspur

Plantain leaves in waves over a lake
Smooth thighs as if in a palace of air
My hand coming through cloud from great distances
Shelters wavering lamp at the foot of your bed
Cuts upward under the sheet to your breasts
Beyond them draws at last to the universal features

To a Meeting by Moonlight, Guler

Ardent in the moon's fullness out you went
To meet the planet's invitation dressed
Fully in white along our silver shores, evening
White wholly as if satisfied—and in that white
You taken for a light moved toward light
Essence in seach of essence, water of water

Night Revelry, Nurpur

Here all is welcome, you are anticipated
With open heart and limbs, entire disclosure
No muslin masking breast or thigh to please
I've multiplied a dozen times rather than
Like a goddess to enclose you in a dozen arms
Take us as one, hold each as if taking the all

Sheltering in Rain, Kangra

Found found again guided by peacock cries
In vast forests of death dark as scudding cloud
You gaze toward, I follow scared to look at you
Until sky rain has fallen, my rain safely bestowed
Parasol over us skylike signifies marriage
My robe your skirt complete the universal circle

Unpainted, Vidyāpati

For as long as I long for you we are two
When you are all my attention we are one
The long forgotten agony of separation from you
In some world above stars flowing past us now
No longer haunts us here as flowers spring up
Which used to flower there and we recognize them

BARTÓK IN UDAIPUR

For John Digby

Golden city on her bed of sand
breathing through towers at the night
immense distance between city and stars
doves passing overhead
taking their upper shining from the sky
their lower from the city

::

No way to staunch flow stop river
feed hungry pour drink down thirsty
drop a coin into every one of a million hands
no way to stop care quench sorrow
no way to end it no way to keep flow
from drowning out eyes no way to finish
no way to grow into salvation no way to end it
roadsign on way to city life is short
do not make it shorter think who awaits us all

::

From all our eyes flows pain
roaring to life with every birth
more births than can be counted on an army's hands
equipped to conquer continents
heroes stand out spearing at one throw
a myriad boars and tigers
with one blood flowing out one sufferance
under dynastic sun sword stroke or parry
calm in sky's eyes profoundly caring

::

Great sails in a sea of crimson
women advancing in greens and blues
flowers of air on a desert morning
gait leisurely pot akimbo high

::

City raising hands to moon
over quiet water birds in hand
among leaves asleep flowers asleep
fisher his blinding turquoise dimmed
a flash of moonlight sets his sapphire
slant fish in beak yet another star

::

To live with one's own face alone
that face for a whole life over whatever
waters night may provide in constant presence
heroes cascade flame-clad on battlefield
women walk with their children into fire
warriors thunder down to inevitable deaths
and lonesome moon with one face only
shines down her equanimity over them all

::

Slinking in poverty by gray green lights
of palaces throned among emerald waters
it used to be our princes inside
exploding fireworks across this lake
now foreigners one with their money
to buy our rings and bangles buy *some* thing
would cost each one of us earth's price
a dozen incarnations or one life's wages

::

Blue god draining all love to him
as his great heart walks over waters
no need of feet wings alone unaided
suspend it at a comfortable height
terns at ankles gulls at knees
over a hunter where he waits for tiger
sudden receiving prey from sky
astonished gratitude

::

Sideslipping warriors in burning clothes
saffron on fire against golden sun
sun's visage peering out of roses
"Ornaments of the State" flowers palaces
what matter which perfume on air
invisible fires in devotional heart
princess in love with a blue forest
youth on cloud enormous and inflamed
blue sword cascading on blind child
crippled for money set in its mother's arms

::

Epic simplicity in dream of stone
raising its walls above our desert
stone of sand and sand of stone
streets running ruby with hot blood
handprints the only archive left by women
whispering windflowers walk into fire
a bruin noise of camels in high distance
night ships asleep over golden dunes

::

Seed towns pink white cerulean
wait for their portraits in rising light
but—lens crash to ground and shatter
with which we saw the stars and closer planets
and studied all the more originalities
blind now we cannot work or must develop
new eyes inside this fire so that whatever burns
with joy or sorrow is but an ornament
of one same state and not a decoration

::

To leave walk out in early morning mist
from dung and dust women arise like flowers
name fourfold origin see fourfold sufferings
which from that day to this under one sun
have not desisted from this land in which
we see love's fourfold origin in pain
including that huge pain inflicted by beauty
planet a lake alone hardly no firmness
colossal cesspool covered with floating diamonds
in the thirty thousand or whatever days
you'll choose as measure of the human life

::

Home floating like a screen in our dreams
light battlements lift desert-colored lake
drained out with blood from all our veins
after a life of miles longest day of year
on which to give thanks for land's blessings
space around land and time for space to heal
as if we were homing there to another star

ASPENS THIS FALL

For Eliot Weinberger & Nina Subin

Power of holy mind:
were it not that Nature obfuscates it with
                    "a temptation of images"...
High over mountain, where voice comes clear
out of the body cavities—voice granted you,
returned in your own voice, the solitude
of every soul who seeks after the kiss:

the aspens turned again,
that fortune ringing silent across sky,
gold waves on mountain ocean—but so silent,
without wave thunder, but with your voice
as if you were a storm, the bush were not in flames,
your voice the bush, heart-bush *never* consumed,
that mountain being now the ladder up to voice—

Gaia, this woman getting gold
among her thighs as if it were a god
and time so short for her receiving.
                    But, suddenly,—eternity;
there is the flash of gold
and the remembrance.

                    How there was a scene,
primal, though innocent, no act but landscape
of a sea you would have looked across...long, long
ago...and somehow recognized (because of cliffs,
beach, boat, perhaps some bathers—no, not a bather,
no human thing—but nature as a whole)
and you were sitting with a person's absence
that half your nature gave you for yourself
so that your mother's son and yours were both as old
as angels smiling on their golden ocean:

Life lets itself be led
in this reverent place, land of cockaigne
loaded with hidden goods—but all for you,
your dining, friends of yours to serve you
without regret. Then the other comes
in some rich conveyance, with retinue surrounded
                           —but in a cloud of peace
you'd never known him show in life, and with a smile
you'd never seen him smile in life—
with great affection greets you as you meet him.

And then, both of you turning—to the third
who had arisen from her golden shower—
the three of you gazing at that landscape
which had become the binding of the book of heaven.
Great peace descending as it only does
in dreams and nowhere else. Last songs
by every great composer sung this moment
more lusciously than ever. Nothing
that you could paint and get away with
in a world of art. Disaster of perfection!

                     (But, suddenly, eternity)
there in the flash of gold: the now,
enriched by past and future disenchanted
(all opulent ambition). A flood beyond
full quantity of fire or water,
rushed down this mountainside—
                     huge ocean of compassion
swamping your heart faster than you could breathe—

                   the all-forgiving view that no-one
can help in any fashion being what they are,
or who they are. And the piece closes
as if the god were dying, breathing his
or her last guess over the magic mountain
and the high mercy of the sea beyond you.

PETALS AND HAIR

For Lee Bartlett

Opening Spring in Fall's embryo:
how shall the past ever come alive
among these plants of another moment,
another life?

              Pass in a nursery
among competing plants of this new season,
consumers pensive, fist at cheek,
(more solitude than any time in action),
moving like sleepwalkers,
choosing their flowers—
sudden irruption as between eyes
yes, almost closed over a dream
of one lost hope from long ago:
world greening—drunken lurch
into an all-untainted vision, brief,
heavenly sky back of the mind,
              the unsuspected home.

So, opening the past, on sudden whim,
fruits thereof brought out and shown
to see if they had rotted, "giving them
airings" he would say—taking the children out
who had grown ghostly with departure
              and giving them that presence,
that life in sound where they had been so silent
such a long time—as if the life had turned
around upon itself, uroboros, begun to recognize
itself as of some value more than passing in his eyes
and in the eyes of others—*this* brought
the quiet crisis on, as you understand it,
as they all understand it, there
              outside the violence.

In the dream, that blossom opening out
was a well-known head, crying from its eyes,
or from your own, it was not certain.
But the following embrace, terribly near,
closer than it had been a lifetime,
                        was . . . what? . . . so . . . *reconciled?*
Even the perfume of that hair,
gray, streaked, sparse on the aging head,
that *far* man's hair, was recognizable,
signaled release from endless slavery,
as long as had it been to time itself,
as to eternity almost, so small the change
                        between that time and always.

Meantime, the new-born roses yet to be
slept on all night, dancing into the dream
from time to time as if they had matured already
—though not a shoot, no hair of green,
lightened the darkness of their sticks. But:
there had been talk of roses in between
him and his audience—that sufficed.

All suddenly came clear—in the still younger
son's turning away from older
because unable to bear
that first departure. Explained the wish,
no, passionate desire, for procreation
and the investment of all love to it—
the very definition of all love as future
and nothing past.
                   And it was all o.k., once
understood—*the* hurt, and once explained,
it could even seem good, that a first bank
should crash and past break down for future
to be whole, pure, love untainted.

Subtle as presence of what he'd known as joy
that long ago, his roses slept under a moon
larger than any he had ever seen in the birth country.
                   One day he would drown more

in that delicate perfume, petals and hair,
glad of the stopping of his sins in time,
since joy had proved again, and joy been proved.

SATURN IN RE THE VENUS CITY (AN ADDRESS WITH NARRATIVE: 1.1.93)

For Bradford Morrow

"In that region, Saturn rules, once thrown from celestial
empire and gods' thrones. Father, his will weighs on
fathers; his protection extending also to the newly born."
—MANILIUS, *Astronomica*

Crass interrupted night, shattered old year,
bombs and trombones to will the new
into submission: up before dawn then,
train howling through the long diagonal
(valley fingers its way toward the sea)
follow dawn-skirts' rise over mountains,
snow mountains, nakedness revealed
bone-white as angels up to dazzled crowns,
gleaming behind those plains and rivers—
our sum of half of history,
their purity in reach still unforgotten
spite aeons of absence,
half his existence, no: over half,
                          stoned on this frozen wind.

Day one of this new year, oh were it first
of all returns to a home city,
impossible and possible, in one embrace,
streets leading everywhere into success—
which is the finding of enchantment
reached by most narrow progress (as it was said
later of door to bliss via proverbial eyes)
walls closing in as if he were intending to—
to err (*errer*)—to wander and be wrong
and this were all he'd ever dared!

The sudden flood of riches given out
as if the city's blood had turned to paint
and the whole globe flared only to be limbed

in paint alone, filtered illusion
to walk in godways. Radiance,
exaltation of angels,
bright on the heart's canals, brushed
never more brilliantly than now: skylarks
hurled out of golden space,
skin-silk reflecting all the light
any god's planet could shed on them
       to fall like manna back.

While the old patriarch come home
looks up in loss of all humanity—
as all out there look up—
for his whole universe
is made to rise, all is salvation
into a painted heaven (merely more radiant
but not improved) over a painted earth.
Titans look down out of terrible mercy
leaving their *macho* goons behind,
their molten amazons, volcano-breasted,
staring earth down—and it is STAY! NOT DIE!
No more departure from this condition
a scarce commodity in fallen worlds:
the faceless mask of happiness forever . . .

Stay here among the city walls,
slimmest of passages to finer grace
than we had shivered from before:
wind out of sea,
her cleansing mercy for any hurt
and end of living coming up
served like unleavened bread
to fathers who have not destroyed their sons
in a far later text than his—
but been their own at whole-life distance:
ram found in thicket that excuse for change,
       and raid on the impossible.

From which last mansions on the dream ladder—
      horrendous god at foot,

judge-devils at the head in pastel robes,
and vacant wings for rent suspended in between:
                         steps, steps, more steps,
legs broken / arms disturbed from sockets—
                              only wings, only flight blessed
to rise or fall above disaster—
child-year torn from the city's great lagoon,
with cloud wafting pale blue and pearl out of the east
                         to clothe our shadows—
and no word else, but *paint* to fill the afterbirth.

Poets came through this marvel, by the quires,
their names dream up and down the walls
refusing to be fixed in their memorials.
But city may yet drown them, all by her godly self.
Thus with this poem—whose draft fell into water
(domesticated sure—but water none the less
left on his writing desk among blue walls
from a spilt vase of flowers)
and nearly drowned and disappeared.
Small news when men are disappeared
all over earth, when cities crumble
less visibly, parks, forests, jungles fall,
mountains themselves from their white heights,
onto this birth day of our last new order.

Not that he will compare—or dare the fates
with neo-classic voice in praise of this princess,
a city state long lost to the live world
doomed like all other stars to barrenness—
but simply to record the correspondences
between a poem and its object when
rare joy gives birth with all her showers
over some single son of a dead light.

MEDITATION: FIRST & LAST TREK, ZANGSKAR

For Kenneth Irby

"*In the early practice the mind is* . . .
In the middle the mind is . . .
At the end the mind is . . ."

—TILOPA

Stone or sand—sand ease of motion,
stone sharp, scree, riprap, obstacle,
falling perpetually down mountainside—
like walk on glass, shard, blade,
cut in the very meatflesh of the foot,
down into bone. The way of heaven,
the way of hell: which can we say is which?
There are, we have agreed, the hells we fear
(much further off the east than this)
and a hell we love. Beautiful hell:
to love and beauty we have contracted,
condemned ourselves. Meanwhile,
mouth dry as hell's part—wind,
altitude—lips almost glued together,
speech all interior of reprobation.
"Immanence without hope." The
immanence is *this*? Blisters on soles,
razors at knees, muscles pulling
against the spine, away from it:
crucifixion of muscles
bunched wrong way up, against the grain.

::

Roses and horse dung.
Later: roses, wild water.
Huge rose bushes against the sky:
rose clouds, rose cumuli
on the blue ether. Extending arms of scent
astounding motherliness of roses,

extending perfume as if to save your mind.
Pass from oasis of salvation
to the next oasis—bury my face
in each bush as I pass
as if collapsing to the motherhood of roses.
These from near-white to neon-pink,
from which all roses sprang
in more familiar countries: rose lineages
in all the universe: there are perhaps
roses on other planets daughters of these?
Pushed into shapes unknown on this?

::

Roses, gods' charity of Zangskar,
soul, distillation of that rock:
I had not thought a flower could save
but, in this nightmare, thought is invalid.
Gentian near-gray in modest isolations,
pearl crowds of edelweiss (hardly mythical),
blue prototype geranium in massed profusion,
limning the barley fields, likewise our fireweed,
forget-me-not playing the register
of light and dark, up/down the mountainsides;
still blue the poppy most solitary of flowers,
round or pyramidal, inspired first plant-hunting
childhood ambitions. The lemon mint,
fragrant drug, stuffed up the nostrils,
rubbed on the mustache . . . Also,
the plethora of birds: redstart,
goldfinch, svelte warbler, doves,
snow doves, pigeons, the little bird
insisting on "tuwitchu" so frequently
it takes you out of mind, numbered among
the fourteen Himalayan kinds of rose-finch.
Choughs play over prayer flags,
dark veering into light and back
strung out from peak to peak between gold roofs.
Perhaps, above the highest pass, a giant span
of lammergeier? Whistling marmots, scurrying voles,

slow yaks and dzos. One crest, crown of the earth
against the sky, carries twelve ibex—
sharp hooves, curved horns of iliad, bugle eyes.

::

But, of these saving graces like the rose,
the other is wild water,
water collapsing from "eternal snows."
Sole water blessing on this land:
rain does not top
the savage peaks to reach it.
For barley, peas and roses, for the
few fields, far apart and sparse,
will let you know how many people
are graced to live in such and such a crease
of the inhuman mountains.
Water to green the land
a month or two before distinction
is blotted out again by new
eternal snows. Wild water singing me
up and down path—this immanence—
waters one dies to drink from
at every meeting, waters would willingly
receive and fill an entire body
thrust into it on a hallucination,
despite stone cut and bruise,
waters I've wanted to remain in,
drink, swallow by uncounted gallons,
even to drown in, as one may drown
in just an inch of water
when breath costs life enough.
So dry the mouth, so dusty
this fine "road," the "only road
to India" as they say,
just some few inches wide,
tortured with every torture of this land,
this madhouse of the gods, bedlam of theirs,
ultimate calcified shit of gods,
bones of more ancient worlds.

::

Also the water of the eternal river
pounding its everlasting passage
like the profoundest message of the soul
into this immanence, water always present,
(corner of eye nearest path's rim)
as foot searches for hold:
so that these gorges are scarcely ever *seen*
on such a trek. Within an inch of life
at any time, walk air, walk water, rock,
from rose to rose to simulate duration,
would dearly like to fall into the river.
Never so royal a procession witnessed
from far to near if such can be distinguished—
at the beginning of the vista, coming;
at middle of it, coming; at the far end,
going, water drowned into going
to come up elsewhere, further on the path
but the same river, song high as wind,
deep as dynamite—ears brought alive, eyes
whiting out to benefit the sound.

::

All night these rivers moving to their ends
invisible; all day the same but visible you think
until the water, running with the mind
becomes the run of it. This earth
in its vast movement flowing
from nought to nought
through all its computations:
you and the earth become indifferent.
There is nothing to do,
no workings to begin, nothing to finish—
all is done for you in that river flow
which is the greatest of the four-fold world.
If I were in the valley gardens,
the dancing gardens of Kashmir
(blood-purple hollyhocks, red poppies,

peonies), where light's white gash
achieves perfection in all wounds,
I would not flow more gently
having kept half my mind
than I flow here with half the loss of it
and with no coat to cover half my body.
Apricot valley; willows of marsh and field
"which I already remember on my dying day"
as if their branches were the orchards
of my own country, were my limbs
(so deeply do they have the reach of home).
Among the broken rock more void
of vegetation than any other rock
this planet knows, wild waters follow on together.

::

There is an island set in a circling sea
of which it has been said (as of the paradise gardens)
"if there be any heaven on this earth
here, here, it's here!"
Cleaning the Zangskar shoes above its beaches—
that these which walked hushed silences
now, white again, might walk such beaches
almost as silent as the mountain passes.
Later this season: no flowers on the sand,
flowers vanished into some ideal springtime
back of the mind. Birds rare:
high loss of wing with loss of hope.
So here to turn away from hope and go
to the vast business—walked on this penance—
of how the light which should be general
becomes imprisoned in countless individuals
so that the understanding is irremediably scattered;
this mind, which could encapsulate a whole,
explodes of it, is exiled into number,
exhausts itself as seas against a beach
no one can see or prophecy the end of,
going uninterrupted round the universe
and out beyond it and herds of other planets—

the beach becoming home, year after year,
to myriads of shells, delicate corpses
borne in to die on it from every ocean.

::

Who came from the warring stars
home to a state of music. To bring on
down the patience. To labor over it,
to enter, although late, the world
at last, though very late, to enter
air around you as if an habitation, place
to feel "freedom" in, and "joy,"
the "immanence-in-joy," caught "as it flies"
without a mineral trace of fear, anxiety,
the sempiternal gnaw of anguish. To move
on rock as sharp as glass all of the time,
to feel it smooth as mind become the mount itself
of "immanence." To have taken a life,
almost the whole of it, to effect this entrance
and to initiate a powerful survival. Reason for "joy,"
even for "praise" who never could see limb of such
or bless intrusion from them in the early life.

"What is it then?" "Is there anything to it?"

BETWEEN A DEATH AND DEATH

In Memoriam: Sasha, Lady Young of Dartington

Moving between a death and death
on every side, at every moment,
at every footfall waiting our end,
miraculously failing us, not finding us,
though we are always there and visible—
what strange, unearthly mist is veiling us
from eye and hand that would transport us
into his home and eat us for his famine
that lasts from the beginning of the world
and never fails him nor is satiated.
Dear enemy, so modest in desire,
he wants nothing but all-of-us to sing
his great, perpetual counterpoint, to noise
all through the universe his triumph over us.
And, in this prosecution, come to birth
and love, we go our ways, evil or just
as the great battle wages us
against each other, men ever cruel
in their terror, too weak to do much else
than his fierce work, his awesome bidding.
So go we always between death and death
all haunting us when life alone should live
in love's great power and death have no dominion
on any kin. Thus am I singing—
who also came to death within this life
and never goes to any life thereafter.

SIEMPRE MAS INVISIBLE (TWO)

For Robin Blaser

"Here is another one!"
a night of passage,
as one might say "a bird of passage" —
but this would be owl or nighthawk.
Garden sleepless in the dark,
stalks bent, silently suffering
night winds of this late March.

On the road to endless darkness,
along this single night of passage:
you want to close your eyes and cannot;
the eyes close with no notion of themselves,
no knowledge of the light
beginning to steal into the room
like a thief of the day to be,
your eyes taken away from you
like all your worthless days
the moment you awaken.

And you have seen—
once, once alone, not custom—
such an astounding beauty in the night
has left you speechless and warm-hearted
toward all of creation;
desperately you try to befriend all things,
germane insistence of the heart,
for the sake of that beauty's eyes
to swear all enemies
are now become your bosom's treasure.
The light in the room has exploded,
a star has been brought to birth
without your knowledge—that fire on the curtain
(in front of your eyes so still in your head there)
is the sunrise of your most mortal day.

And you wake on that morning
with an atrocious sense of loss
as for the friend of your life
never met, never to be met, again
robbed of that exquisite sister in the dream,
soul of your soul.

You were still thinking of going to sleep,
you were still thinking of some benefit,
wretched trustee of every human loss,
when it was morning.

RED BANNER'S WHEREABOUTS

For Robert Kelly

Now where is my red banner moving to
on this electric wind—hotter than ever day
can be remembered in these parts—or on this moon,
against the blacking out of hope,
our certainty that to be happy is to share
in the belief of one another's happiness?

    Voices all around us on these winds,
        as if in a battle of flowers
            on a coast used to be fabled for joy.

    Simple acceptance: I give, I take, you take . . .
        I have given to the limit of my shame,
        to the name you gave it, saying: yes, take,

but we are losing ourselves in the competition,
unable any longer to distinguish our own message:
    edge is serrated,
    we cut our tongues alone
        on the extremities of our own truth. Where
is my banner gone, or going where, that fire,
        as we sink down the mountain
into earth's bones?

    Presage of a body so huge
it is impossible to grasp it with the mind
unless you move mind up, by some mechanism,
set of jumped steps it has never experienced:
    up/down: ant is dog-sized,
        star sits, a diamond in your hand,
            earth's bones shift to another focus
            of such high dividend
    terror blackens your teeth sudden as fire,
        floods in your mouth sudden as waterfall.

To go down the great spine
as if the middle country had been lost eons ago,
paradise preserved there,
locked between major arteries, invisible from them,
leaving all other voices in those arteries,
            jazzing and jabbering along them,
                    my poor, sad, saturated nation!
But on that center, famed for beauty alone,
the voice you looked to die with might reappear,
            sound again, soar contented.

                        And no matter
they ran out of names to name the mountains with
            so that three giants in a row
                        are coiffed with the titles of
three *petite* colleges back east
as if the west had whelmed its iconographers!

Clouds still roil above these storm kings—
blancas as the fathers called them
                        from their snow veils—
don't let the tongueless fuck with them,
force them from pastures out to highways
where they'll lose voice which on mind depends.

Oh where is my red banner moving to
wavers so close to my face in the home gardens
I cannot see it—nor can it see me
        (as they once said "to see/to know"
            being the ultimate in sapience)
but now, among these foreign voices, as I turn
to gain release, there is its move from wall to wall,
            flaring against the white . . .

If you but knew that land!
                    I buy myself a music,
purchase permission here of you,
                    dear friend and that,
to walk once more, as if angelkind,
                    in the garden of language—

where is my banner now
        to go before me: revolution,
            no longer mother—everbride
                something I can depend on,

abides like city parks do, in childhood cities
prolific shops, yes, in childhood cities,
where the books came from, cacti, stamps perhaps,
        I don't remember now—
            when uncle Oedipus walked back into our town
once in a century . . .

It should be possible
to write forever
without pen scorching paper
                all of the time,
to keep distinguishing a true volcano
from sullen lava of the dispossessed:
all of these voices, breaking silence singly
(or all at once and cacophonously)
        which will never empower
                one midnight courier.

Promise like shards of glass on a broken floor.
        Can we start out again?
                Slide down the mountain's breastbone
into the gully where they build a town,
        re-build a whole old town
in which to gamble the new?
        They'll bring up from the highway, east and west,
televized players, chips and strumpets,
deejays' asses, dank trombones.
                It is imperative to get beyond
        this cancer of the language. Can we leave?
Keep to the central road back to our home
        with the red banner forward on the hood,
                letting them know who's coming?

Chaffee County, Colorado

AN INTERVAL

For Edward & Jennifer Dorn

An interval
in the bowels of time. A crossroads
among intestines
where the swelling of life,
either up or down, may access sound.
Where desire
generates power, shorted these many months,
accelerates to confidence, formats
the possibility of voice to music. It is
a move toward the recognition of
individual doom and its acceptance
at the same time as rage
battles against it, longing to torture
with as much pain as possible
selected files of victims.

The burden here: abyssal appetite
for rest from self's desire—all
that can fabricate an individual,
urge, will, push, purge
of all encodings else than the one goal in sight
that makes me such and no ways like another
to finalize the one in its "eternity."
My ancient enemy, the game of chance—
its arbitrary siting of specifications,
isness of is, its quiddity, such that
the vision never for a moment wavers—
this random bliss will desolate me whole.

Look at this city long enough to see
as clearly as your "soul" can ever
thousands on thousands
of single wills scripted for lone agendas.
The anguished knot

of each such singularity
(behind the similarities each is entrapped in
by cultural convention)
throttles the viewer's own and makes him long
for passage from this prison.

                         At last,
lining the street I work for miracles
even the single flower on a bush of flowers
so numerous it seems the bush is "heaven"
afflicts me with a misery as fathomless as ocean,
where even "gods" are swallowed.
The bee, to swell her thighs with honey,
passes within a sigh to one more flower and yet
another, multiplies monads, raises the paradigm
of color-switches: pink, deeper pink, red, orange,
yellow—though, thanks, not structure here:
content but never form—or we would lose our minds.

Mind is the question then again, and yet
again: not all your flights, nor your avoidances,
running from telling me the one thing needful
to my salvation, can mute that riddle:
facing that sphinx being my whole profession.
The medication will take its month to function—
meantime the body senses time's insinuation
of fevers (wretch & shiver) and those same
angers whose fierceness shakes me like malaria
against all matter—even the things
man can do nothing with, as the philosophers
one time advised: do what you can against
what you control, but things not in your power
you must perforce ignore. Yet, time and time again:
how shall I visit the hundred thousand things,
assimilate the hundred thousand passions,
how read the hundred thousand books
before, on all the libraries of "paradise,"
          a sign: "closed for the whole duration"?

                              "Dear God," and then
                     the "poem,"
the "poem" in all this: what will become of it
among the mindless swells who run the business
of sing-consumer-sing this *fin de siècle*?
Role of self-swollen slammer deliquesces;
all who run trade: voice, commentary, voice,
recorder of the voice, who writes it down,
publishes it, broadcasts it wide, reads and rewards
and re-remembers it: all slime, foul, all despicable,
all bottom line on culture's bottom line—
even the rats and vultures run the polity
will not bother to taste let alone feed on
though happy to make lip quiver to lip
at the elections in defense of "art" . . .

Forget the wording "poet." Call me a
"hermit" who would depart the planet
as it stands now, ready to cataract
into the coldness of the other spheres,
and move into a glasshouse all my own
on another star. Then to begin again
asking myself, as my own "sphynx" this time,
whether the one will multiply out there
or yet remain the unity I so desire.
                     Still, still,
I sight no other "gods." Nothing to fish
me into a communion. Suspect, why even now,
dust back to dust sleeps everlasting sleep
without the pretty: "resurrections." Then there
I plunge, respect me mind you, enter into
my "origin"—and timelessly,
tail curled around an emerald sargasso,
a pregnant myth of the primordial ocean,
discover me inhaling songster multitudes.

There now: a curtain has been drawn
back from the skylight of this instant.
Quiet: the peace of made. Or better still,
the peace of the unmade.

You, other you, reader
of auspices and horoscopes, you undiscovered cosmos,
you passing in the single night of all our breath,
you, love, now ever multitude, but with the face
all warriors before have fallen for in time—
blessings, green daughter, on your closured eyes
as blessings I will beg of thee, now, momentarily
                    as you enplane the mind.

Swallowing molten lead
does much to rouse an appetite for life.
As for the rest, honor the bee
passing from dream to dream,
in her loud unconcern. Killer
of killers, alien of aliens,
fool of fools—I who have sung this,
my grief is done, just this one instant
for a brief repose—
"I" have the right to "I" again at last
until the monster tears me once again
with his saw teeth, the black bile flowing free.

THE WISDOM ROSES

For Peter Cole

From desert into desert
the fragile vein
stretched on the sun's circumference
                    ready to burn
but so full of iced blood
                    it is protected—
and in this equilibrium
          the understanding passes
from root to trunk and out to branches
where the rose sits much higher than itself
          existence perching on existence
like hawk on prey
                    to contemplate a meaning.

          That there was something, back of this palisade
          so high no one could see or guess
          as the trains passed from west to east . . .

No book will ever hold, no dictionary
               spell out exactly
the passage back from bee to aether:
that bee in burdening the rose
                    provokes a paradise of gardens,
greens out the ocean which had thought itself
                    greener than all creation
and then the aether with its eyes as blue
as the deep skies demented on our deserts
                    distills creation's best defined
and archangelical desire.

          . . . as the trains passed from east to west
          a something like a camp where lives were broken
          back into numbers in the sub-degree . . .

298

Lying inside the dream
          for almost ever
that opening we call the past
along the tightrope into morning:
how much I miss thee golden daughter,
          never known city,
inheritance of peace—
          my never visited,
unseen and unremembered, underprophecied
          house built of bone and solid blood
so soon to liquefy.

          Now all is gone, all traces taken out
          blamer and blameless buried in the ruins—
          no one would think of chewing bitterness.

How I have understood thee
          golden city,
not with a hillside charity
but in the water realm,
          the sea deep under sand
into which flow these rivers
banked eden after eden with wild roses.
How sing thee in strange lands
          and not by light be eaten
if it should pass we die for brothers
          down from the hawk with bloom in beak,
descending back from aether into life?

the architextures

For Janet Rodney

Isn't it the end now, isn't it the way you come home as if you were not coming, as if you were staying down and were going to eat of that food for all time, what is it, the amaranth seeds, or poppy seeds, or the marigold seeds, something intolerably like that, and would be satisfied to stay down there forever, without anything to say to yourself in this new tongue, this novel we are trying to talk up here, or to say for yourself, to tell us in unwearying detail, what it is that our time needs to know that is so close now to finishing without ever having had its say?

Isn't it the truth now: that we no longer surmise where we are? That the art no longer knows where it is, that the art is repeated over and over, that the city has to be abandoned to its aging, a brand new city going up beside it, to explode into this century which is so late in manifesting? Manifesting its particular commitment of the environment to the setting and the setting to the environment, so that we have at last, what is it, a story told, a narrative in building?

So that you ask yourself, looking out of all the windows of the dead, one after another coming to each window, parting the curtains, shrouds over the windows' eyes, looking out onto that void, trying to make out the contours of the new city—but with the angle always wrong, the new buildings being just out of eyesight, just out of the field of perception—you ask yourself: what is that being, that very pale being, are we that being, that ghost almost, what is that being trying to come up very slowly, into the upper air, and is she making it? Have we determined it is a she, is she making it, or an it, or a he, or, is, she, making it, or we? Is she reaching that upper air, is she coming up here to say something to us, is it true that at last she is coming home, is she coming home, is she home, is this her here beside us? Looking now back down in the opposite direction, proud of her raising herself to this unlooked for stature, of having made something out of herself, and out of *you* into the scenario?

How is it that this man of music reaches all the world, by coming up out of his own earth and going into all the various territories, taking that music with him? For it is not like language which stops you, like a door you cannot go through — but like a transparent curtain, a veil, you go through with the greatest ease. And here is the heart of mankind beating from one end of a great city to the other which is the whole earth now, where all roads spider over the planet, roads so wide you can see them from any other planet, however far away, and how marvelous it is that all this could be done with music.

It is also true that the music had to come out of the graveyard: opening the iron gates of the graveyard, every one of the stones within cleaned, polished, the names memorialized, flowers arrayed under every name, under innumerable winter snows: so you issue from that place and the understanding that the place gives you flows without impediment into the music. So that everywhere you go, they bring you tributes of flowers, books, pictures and everything that summons up the holy name of music and everything in the roundabout universe that nurtures music: memories, thin and thick sadnesses, knowledge, disaster, eschatology — and it is all full to explosion with a love of life which almost sweeps you out of existence and into . . . into *what*? Into what else is there but this existence? What else is there but the distant sound of justice?

And she, does she remember stones moving when the music played, animals leaning on their paws, attentive to those strains? Remember the people there, quietly beginning to dance and does she see those birds in the trees swaying, those fish in the river meandering by, sinuate this way and that to the music? Look up at the far star fields sensing them, can it be possible, move into time to the music and, moving thus, generate their own music, and does she, seeing all this, finally know whether home is on this earth and is she joyous thereat? Go up to the lead dancers and bow to them, and then, secure in and of her own place, begin to lead the dance in a quiet kind of triumph as if any time in which she might not have led it had been forgotten, so much forgotten that they will say of it: look, this was nothing but a dream? Something which, pulling it apart, you'd call a vanishment?

Where is the edge of the new and where do we go in this immensity which tells us we move from one place to another, instead of moving inside one place which is always recognized? How do we know that we go from the known to the unknown, and has this new place not always been inside us since the beginning, that we go from the safe to the unsafe, the adventurous, the chivalrous, the quest, and are not draped in the safe, hidebound, cloth of gold, tailored its thousand pieces like to a robe of abdication? When is it that we are in our landscape, full of rural preoccupations, and that we then move toward the urban threshold, manifesting a city's future wholesomeness in the traffic patterns of our brains? Is this *città nova* or *città antica* and who can guarantee it either way? Out of the mouths of angels at every gate, flaying passersby as they are chased into this agglomeration, what is it that chorals assent and willing servitude, glows out in a breath of fire toward those latter distances, the maps of everything we have deserted forever?

How did we stand still and how then did the whirling universes stop flashing past us small as the daughters of our eyes? To grow, outward into that dense immensity like to an ocean crystallized, a frozen summation of geography, giant vision of every planet in the galaxy, galaxy in the cosmos: how did our stillness breed this colossus—and why do we ever bother to read another single word (or to write one) where there is enough here to last in the diction of it for inexhaustible lifetimes?

Where was she: still or running? Frozen statue of a running girl, frozen in bronze and in ice covering the bronze—that day in the park which taught us childhood, chilled even more as the girl that was perpetually running away from us, flying away from her frozenness in space and in time: we that were supposed to be the ultimate freezing agent, the megalomanic oppressors and paralyzers of everything sentient? When, already, inside there, turning around that very moment at the apex of flight, there was a body, hers, flowing out of the metal, curving, to begin the run back toward us, to return to this terrestrial island, to come back once again and forever to this home, at the center of everything, whose image all along the paradox of her flight she had never been able to flee from, had never shaken from her, never let go of, nurtured like the vision of a paradise to become?

Who are we that fled the thousand lives we did not lead in order to escape the very one life that we were destined for? Who after years, centuries, eons of fleeing, suddenly, in one moment, in a garden, a public park perhaps, felt cornered by that one true life, reeking at us from everything surrounding: trees, bushes, lawns, benches, people sitting there, children playing with hoops, skittles, or little yachts on the pond, windows of houses overlooking the park, potted nightingale-flowers tucked into balconies, servants living under the roof and looking down onto the park, wishing they could take the air out there—and we were overcome by a smile so vast we had not enough mouth to smile it, with all our teeth shining like white suns, the way they shine in the new countries, on the new beaches, *where the new nations rush along the strand in their joy?* Who went to those countries at the time of their "liberation" and asked of them whether men still feared death now that they were part of ever-lasting life—to come home saddened, reporting they still feared death and that the human condition had not changed?

Who wrote innumerable words adding up to something we felt a part of, in whose reality we sank with coolness, gratitude and the immense comfort of those who have at last found home, whereas all the countries sur-rounding us withered into a perpetual frost and the houses we had lived in became encased in ice, the memories of those who had known us mirrored over like ponds in winter—geese only shattering the silence, turned south over our frozen decoys?

How did she then, belonging to the people for whom mind is an insult and not the ultimate glory of our state; how did she come down, suppos-edly to comfort us, with her hoops, bangles and rings, prodding us intermin-ably into jumping, into leaping through these rings that she thought were fire, which would test us and prove us and make us into man—but only lifted us aloft from the true conflagration, flew us above our burning sense of the one life lived, turning liver to salt, spleen to white flour, seeming to challenge the lilies of the field, white on the white expanses, their whys and wherefores, their lovely concentration into falls—of cowardice, of petrified desire?

Stress on seven intense from plethora of clocks. Had he been there another hour would they have stressed time too? For now, weight lifts from a familiar recital: organization withers to rest. Maternally for him it can do nothing more. Weight sinks back then—and flowers of glory waver on the abyss instead. His radical surprise! Force of decisiveness! It is as if they were names: in his mind, will it not be so with their perfumes? Letters of these names hard to abscond with, yet he has known of their alphabets always. It is only that you have to follow the aleph with the beth—and so forth down the years. He found it very needful to seize this hour before such buildings claimed him. You arrived in that somnambulant pink air Pleasance was famous for— although it was at least seven of evening and you knew you had been granted into another world.

Grace of that new root which is so old in him, it is his anchorage: he always cuts from it! Here he is, so clearly assisting his own birth. Maternities pour down afresh from all his ceilings; showered with infants of all sexes as if in a squall of flowers. Is it not the truth these people mastered size as no others have? Seize the hour! For buildings here are larger than any made in his own era. He may run the danger of disappearing into them forever, dissected in small corners no one would ever recover. Buildings smiling down on small, cross towns around them, huddled from roof to roof, swarming with dwarf contentions: have you noted how they speak to each other in streets and *piazzas*, these folk, as if there were time for nothing other than to be violently born? Whereas his people! As if manifest destiny existed in silence—unspoken, unspeakable, the very alpha of wealth itself! As if they had not precluded wealth by concern for no other repression!

Is it not frequently that "to write" is an act which is not to be followed by "to read," unless a "to read" were to be experienced as a "to write"? But this would alleviate from the original "to write" would it not? If such there ever was, would it not? But they do not know that there was such an original ever. Thus do they not retreat over and over? Until they reach no beginning— and, in that circumstance, come to understand there is no other life?

ARC25: 89

I. M. Franz K.

He has permission of morning to reach evening. Massively closed of late, doors of eternity open again: would *you* enter them and be lost? No, he prefers uncertain stay outside gigantic gates he knows to be for everyone alive: excepting him. He has begun to think she is a strange one to take a man crazy with stars into her house. But she can nurse her comfort: he's no astrologer. Distrusts each single one of those maddened lights. Sure none will ever actually come down, or stretch to reach him. Suddenly, remembers trains which started out from a known place, arrived another, stopped at a whole bunch in between. As long as they do that is all he'll ever ask or ever will require. Obsessional. He who wrote in passionate friendship a full year after meeting—but had not thought to send some sign between: what *do* you *do* with such unerring lovers?

"If only he'd slip off into the light of heaven" she had thought—but he would not. Here is a whole *noblesse* fiercely believing he has them by the root. Constrained to correspond with him each once a day; call him each once a week; lard him with gifts, honors, awards each once a month, take him to town for ice cream once a year: and, *no* he sits as lone as fossil locked in rock. With that degree of dryness you could not spark with matches however hard you tried. It is the flame-proof dryness of the pharaohs.

Then, he would remember palaces standing in their own sweat of summer light, roof sculptures turned this way and that—some talking at the void, some versing with each other, always one at least singing, a few avoiding others, a couple so completely self-enwrapped, their steady gazes gashed fontanas into the cloth of heaven. From which new stars shone down. That fair rotunda famous throughout the world. Still, he dwells on in disbelief. Stars shine on down, ignoring palaces, preferring in cold wisdom a vernacular landscape. He is appalled at his fate: being a great believer—sometimes, he thinks, an only believer.

His hills and valleys stand around his outing. From century to century, looks up, cognizes fortune. Clear north wind day. Waters dream over all, sea both in sky and under sand—unperishing, uninterrupted fire. Sun shoulders shadow, slant falls across both pine and juniper. Out of silence, wisdom bats softly, always occult at the head of the eye, blinking among her foam of feathers. Tan feathers and the rising horns. If he forget both fire and origin of breath, he grounds among the hills and valleys. How stands this fortune he glares at day by day, unwilling to collapse into the deathful?

Absence of name, void as fields between stars. This place astonishing. Pure field. Mile upon mile of field (every conceivable direction)—plus up and down, plus center. The farthest place he'd ever come to. He did not know; he was not sure; he'd have to look for proof—but then again he might have found, might have discerned, the treasure island. That this perhaps at last, this might have been, the innermost, most immanent, core of his darkness. In the midst of which, with nothing round it for a thousand miles, they'd built a Center of Centralized Studies the like of which no one had ever seen. But, studying in which, he could not move at night a few suburban blocks down to his home.

Womb as restraining matter: flower of flower as such we are bound to, lining from which we float into this birth. Inside? Seed of itself, exciting him, slaking the soul out of enamorment which then can summon her and kneel her down before him. Petals distill a dew to fall from crown to root of darkness, then to flow up again to other petals at body's ultimate, most diminutive mouth. Where sun awaiting beggars the trick. Of she what has been eaten is a field of produce sown from her every pore. She drenches out his dew into the earth—and with it all attachment to the withered flower. Freedom! He'll copyright the thing so that it stays a secret, no fodder for the vain. Only their bees come alive, self-born of their own honey. Patrivore and Matrivore devour each other in showers of fine laughter.

Ted Enslin

Sure there must be a place from where you can depart. From where you go into your head toward that other place. That other place in which the where and when are made. In which you spend most of your life pursuing where and when. In which all those you know—almost without exception—are desperately lost. Or where they hardly know, or you, that all are lost. Or that this place, so like it seems not other, is yet indeed the same as the departure place. There stands the wheel of heaven. Its multitude of mansions between each of its spokes. There you go up or down accordingly. Also you never move.

And our eyes are so blind, the why rattles its cages like a raucous bird to so many a why. If eyes could see, there would be no why—only assent. Up we go into the mountains—feet accumulate by thousands; breath comes short on short; just tying up a shoelace you collapse from great heights. Up there the prayer-flags slap birdless air, songless altitude. Though there is always a raven to croak what seems the time and chat you up with some small prophecy. Silently you look around for your ram caught in his thicket. But the thorn holds you—no horn visible.

Eyes of turquoise water far down among the valleys look up at you in wonder. You wonder back. The rivers move between valley and valley among mountain boxes. She of all compassion with all her hosts: streams from your fingernails. The where, the when, the why carried toward the sea—far off and more besides in yet another country. Souls in our mouths locked in by these rough roads remind us that we have no place to go. Except out of the place of where and when. Back to that place from which we had departed: should not all travel be immediate return?

For him who struggles whole lives through and never rests. Though late beginner, aged on meeting with the kingdom, though most about to die just when salvation dawns, that farthest father of a western wall, where sons of every manner can go down and where sweet mother ever points the way, that is the nation he desired. *"An end is come, the end is come; it watcheth for thy health of mind, behold it is come. The morning is come unto thee,"* o thou poor citizen! *Thou* art the nation wedded, citizen, none else, no other voice, o my poor friend, my fathermotherland! So do I dream of thee, on that far side of any wall, having become there in my very song, that manner consecrated.

Who then had brought himself to the edge of drowning in that sand, of choking in that river, where all the good and all the evil he had done had come to similar conclusion: that it was all of one cloth, of the one water, like thread to thread, like drop to drop—had anyone committed to a pleasant end, a lovingkind conclusion? Had it ever been said that love would be returned, another cheek returned, that simply on account of love, you would be loved as well? Nonesuch and nonpareil. There on the grave it could be read, graved on the tombstone out of rock and marble: *"You who are radiant, look down on my desire, the sweet boy of my youth, no longer desolate, for he is come back home"* and the dove's voice is heard, like liquid honey running on the land! And answer right below: the love I offered is *not* returned, I die alone a multitude.

Ah she was young, the country, the sweet land, with laugh like music in throat's depth, a smile in every word as it might issue—or merely be suspended right behind her eyes! How other nations had grown old and sorrowed and then died—for loss of empire, dried up for lack of oceans to reconquer—but she, the everyoung, rebuilt herself anew, in every epoch, in every pore, rose artery and vein. Had she not been desired, clung to as the embodiment of the great tongue, *the voice*: had ruthless man not taken her to wife who owned the land she burnished—and all its sounds? *All* given up for her, *all* sacrificed, as much as half a life thrown down the drains of the old world to gather up the new! And now the price: to rot on your own altar, with not a bird in sight to devour your guts!

Lift the veil. See the body underneath. See the born beauty of the day revealed that started with such hope. There is so little time before night falls. In my ending is despair said the philosopher: lovers denied him. Despair—but let it not appear so. Appearance is the be-all and the end-all in our work, is it not so? We are the men of confidence, her hopeful suitors, her loving cavaliers. No: see the day and tell of it as if it were the finest of your life, as if many a day were similar to it, as if you knew contentment. And could provoke it. Good morning, Grandfather: to the pinyon tree. Good morning, Grandmother: to the juniper. So would it be throughout day, week, month and year, the learned lifetime. Desire would make it so.

One day the anger will have ended and love will have shone through. All screens will then have fallen. Because you will have known so long our tragedy, our quest so desperate, our almost irretrievable disaster, the love will have shone through, the sad fate shared. Nothing will have been promised in return. It is not possible to set out loving and to expect an answer to that love; there is no guarantee of it, any of it. The love is not returned. You die there long and last without return. Only that anger should have gone—and absolution. That nothing dark remain upon the head of the beloved when no return is made. That the beloved maintain distance and solitary splendor. This as the only task of hope.

She will have broken through at last. Millennium on millennium—and no sign of her. That head in darkness, that miraculous body, those feet, the wave treaders, who walked on water. The miraculous mind, invisible, thinking its planetary thoughts; that mother of all things: created, uncreated, born, coming to be born, not being born for ages, and to be born right at the end of time. Her laughter falling through these clouds, rising from steam over the waters. Step after step, step after step, the movement steady, not up, not down. Yet, a slight up, mostly suggestion, the way we apprehend it, there is no other. The veil is drawn over despair, falls on that death head, closes those vacant eyes. Despair no longer present. Spring in the famished mind, the leaves starting to form, infinitesimal, the flowers coming up over the graves. No longer hope, no longer love. A presence only. A constant presence.

three letters from the city:

the st. petersburg poems,

1968–1998

ONE: THE NAMES RETURN

In Memoriam: Musya T.

To be writing to you
            fifty years beyond death,
        as you used to write,
giving all, asking nothing,
one yet so "difficult" of reputation,

who needed all, received so little
            except your diamond voice,
you who had seen most die, most
            everyone of the old world,
the world before the first occasion:

the "never yet," the "always so,"
the borderless "already there" —
where, on the other hand,
the "spirit" nameless, undefined,
gave to your joy the strength of

cataracts falling like precious stones
from your skull's skyline,
            you for whom death
could sound like life, and suffering
        flower in smiles of pleasure . . .

How we loved *that* world,
            that recognition
of everyone around us:
        a room
in which a body could survive,
            a spirit breathe,

so earth would not be trembling all the time
(dropped by a mother goddess
            into a blind abyss),
a memory could revel in itself
not, as down here, having to drink this place
and then, again, drink that,
            granted very short stays
then thrown into the streets again:
uncounted coffees, innumerable teas,
"My God, we are not camels to be drinking all day!
And all night too—since there's no dark
but everlasting day in desiccated exile!"

Speaking the language
            of lineages ago
language of exile
no longer recognized:
            is *this* our language?
It is, it *is* the language,
but it has grown to wood,
it misses the word "soul,"
            and everything dries up
around that absence.

There are no fathers left,
            no mothers, siblings,
not a single parent. Orphans
            move into dawn,
command the sun to rise.
It has forgotten how to rise:
the trade of following the sun
no longer known nor served.
Immense darkness prevails: only
the leaves' caress along a cheek
as you pass, going home,
constricted tributary streams
or streets like snake lungs
granting you the way.

Song, the monastery,
for one, two at the most,
and the other to be a sister soul,
our giving up of all the information
had made the world seem precious,
transformed it day by day:
since to work wondrous change
is often just to leave a new space void
            of outworn furniture.
Smoke lifts off our days:
what we had thought of as fresh
is but a road to repetition.

            Of neglect make a wall
stronger than stone,
of the spear in our sides
make a wall of steel,
flatten it, spread it out, will it
into a wall of steel.
            No happiness there, true,

            but *Freiheit!*
To wear the badge of oneself
being the servant of no one,
that "self" hardly ever present,
gone into orphanhood—
and suddenly, time which had seemed
            so short so long a time,
time once again is endless
            as close a model on this side . . .
                        eternity itself.

            Who walk by the ocean
looking for "the meaning of our days":
the ocean all one taste,
            one waste of tears, one flavor—
it could be all,
it could be part—you would fall off of it
            and drown in space—

but no! There is one earth at the far end,
           pure land on which to build
                   the city as it was of old
according to the everlasting image
tall now, defined, inhabited, triumphant.

And here is where we live,
you who becomes the city, you invited by
I citizen of these immeasurable futures —
with every past redeemed and safely anchored
around the void of nothing lasting ever,
down to that river as broad as the sea,
which is the sea already on the face of it,
           forcing our city's arms and thighs apart,
advancing wider shorelines
                   into the mother ocean.

Now time enters the city's centuries
much as the sea enters its walls
both from an immemorial *tremendum*
as we invest the city with our small histories
which is nevertheless the all we ever have
from the same source working the same desire.
As names flow back into the city
from years no one had overcome
to overlay new names pasted onto the streets
and squares, parks, gardens, palaces
from times some would rather forget
                   and cannot altogether.

Remembering your destiny
           translucent polity of stone
struck with the death of millions:
           blood hardens into granite,
                   brains into bone,
the bones dancing in robes of lace with red embroidery
           red/white nightmare of nations . . .

May the sea be so vast, it drowns you out
translucent city before you join the crowd
of faceless cities tamped by consuming mobs
and robber rats squeezing out of the sewers,

may all solutions break to the ravaging waves
and be the last of cities, still, serene
and sapphire at the bottom of your ocean
far down, far down, jewel of memory

rather than fall as so many have
to tides of hardening excrement—
and may your shadows linger in our memories
like clouds over the rivers on an august day . . .

To be in love with you
                    like fifty years ago,
        to write to you
on a fogless day, dazzled with clarity,
as if your blue cathedral had fallen through our eyes,
and winter snowdrifts had prematurely toppled
to fold our city on all its conquerors!

SEVEN: THE FUNERAL, AUGUST 10TH

In Memoriam: Sasha B.

Marked of fate
to lay himself bare into the world
    for the starved of spirit—
perhaps the whole of himself is demanded
and therefore he dies early
for nowhere else does the word
    become bread and stone as with us here.
And therefore also will there be no complaint
as to his fate: for he is listened to
    for good or ill.

While we are still in waiting: wait under glass
tears frozen on the lower lashes,
    needles of ice on the astounded air
floating like dragonflies in summer light.
From which window to look out
    on the daughter of the river,
from which eyes: his or the whole's?
    In the intolerable silence,
looking out far over to the city walls
    where he shall choose his grave.

To save her! To save her from the night!
Who? the Girl? or Revolution?
    He cannot decide . . .
        In truth the Girl and Revolution
have always been one and the same for him.
And friendship? Its very nature is obscured
when everyone is more like everyone
and numbers grow beyond endurance.
Tasks multiply and every soul, alive or dead,
    raises the wall of work,
        the wall of "being busy,"
and time no longer moves from day to day
    but year to year

                    with nothing in between.
It is the "soul" which is the prison!
                    Give up "soul"!
Of course it will not stomach
                    the word "compassion."
It is the body which will share its love
and suffer in its language with the multitudes.

        Tormenting sense of youth,
        of being at the beginning
when there is no youth left,
                    and has not been
                          for countless years.
It is a promise given at the dawn
on the first day of the remembered era
—i.e. the beginning of time for our purpose—
that keeps us moving and refreshes us
though body always wears the color gray.
No! rather absence of all color,
color draining away, until a ghost
moves in your place vacated in this land
which never took to you, never allowed you flesh,
never gave you the incarnation you desired
and yet for which you held that promise,
kept it as the one focus of attention,
your one desire, stone polished for a lifetime.
        But you abandoned it, in lieu of an existence ...
            You done. You through with it. You over.

                                        All the sounds

have gone silent. Can you not hear
there's no such thing as sound again
or any more? Others go blind
                    but he is deaf to music.
It would be blasphemous
to try by any reasoned method
to call back sound in soundless space.
                    He used to think
he could hear music off the furthest shore,
beyond the last house in the city—

music of a great day, festive rebirth
                        of all he'd hoped for.
He kept this thought alive for lifetimes
transmitted hope to youth when he had lost it,
                        kept that last bloom alive
as long as there was light, sunlight and water.
        A great wall's up:
                Music has died.
                        He can hear nothing.

You think it done,
the interminable business,
because you have won a lifetime's struggle
you think you can now buy and play with toys
        for the rest of eternity—
but it has *not* ended, it is nowhere near
                        ended yet,
it will come again, the reckoning
it will reappear as long as time lasts
                        always, always.

        He walks alone.
Friends and admirers several paces behind
as he goes to his lecture
deaf to the city, deaf to history.
They dare not overtake him,
they walk with him for the last time
                        clutching books and flowers.

Similar to other cities, river-crossed,
river-transfixed it seems to them
and yet there is an aspect of space here
        they could not comprehend
        until they understood
how wide the river was,
that it was not the river entering the city
with bridges stretching to their utmost power—
but entering the city from another world
                        it was the ocean . . .

The sea received him with a giant breath.
At last he knew how to give up resistance.
Rivers, in love through all their traveling,
                                    expect that sea.

THIRD LETTER FROM THE CITY, 1998

*Не мелькнет ли там на бледной
черте, отделяющей синюю пучину от серых тучек,
желанный парус, сначала подобный крылу морской
чайки, но мало-помалу отделяющийся от пены
валунов и ровным бегом приближающийся к
пустынной пристани . . .*

—М. Ю. ЛЕРМОНТОВ

I

City of patience:
      paradisal Hades.
Emperor enthroned:
      too many palaces—
and the entrances
      so diminutive
you cannot see the lackey
      sells you your ticket:
only a claw, out and in.
Lining of ancient gloves
worn by the lords of old
      fit to my hands.
Here, as in dreams of youth,
      a student prince again,
heart-close to friends,
      seeing them at least
once, twice a week, or even
      running into them
on streets desire dictates.
Yet, in this circumstance,
      desire the devastator,
poisonous dye,
      flood-cloud through
all degree. Stones heavy,
      ice heavier,
whole city one vast skating rink,
tall ships marooned here, there

as if it were bridges that moved.
An immense weight of darkness
no scales can ever define:
tidal waves from the sea
      as if from other worlds.
What *is* this darkness
hanging like sails from masts
of these lone fire-towers on the ice?
      Today the light came out
between layers of darkness,
outlined fortress spires
      royal eye's needles
flaring like beacons round the port,
      reporting back to all the desks
of the royal prerogative.
      Here in my teens, my twenties,
living a time I have not yet experienced
      because of running backward
into a multitude of royal maws.

II

Ah God, I am asleep, I dream!
The time it has taken to come here,
      to reach this place,
woven out of heart sinews
      (will it continue to beat?
will it be able?)
      preempts all time remaining,
makes rescue of all city memory
the most imperative of all our tasks.
      Never again to wear the badge
of a city prince in splendor,
      I cannot pay the tax,
price of admission to the court,
the ransom is enormous,
      out of all proportion.
          All the king's offices,
museums, *kunstkammern*, zoologies,

his mammoths baked in ice, his curiosities
(infants pickled and bottled as in cures
for worlds gone terminally sour):
all these failing to pay for my redemption.
   Time to go, way past time to go!
and yet he will not, this emperor,
  the sweet will to change
has turned to ambergris in him
   and will not exit.
     He will not abdicate
to rise into the upper circles.
Long leads in ice run to the fortress
and back again up to the bridge
   low slung over the river.
The ice piles up upon itself,
      graying with age.

III

My spirit
  a thousand-legged horse,
each leg an anxious dream,
  leaps the divide
twixt Arctic and Antarctic,
Europe—America
  with Asia in between,
defining Empire. Crowds,
faces set, waking from slavery
but still unsmiling,
  up from the ground—
migrating clouds.
Pit opened up in time:
all of remaining time packed in,
  my eyes have abandoned me
they can no longer see into the future—
  distance has shrunk
to the last speck between these walls,
  the offices are closed
for the duration.

To do or not
no longer signifies—
		what I accomplish
fades into world-wide webs of deeds
		like ghostly skeins
transparent as the threads of water.
			Gone here,
gone over water to another shore
from which only to start
		is but to end in heaven—
and yet everyone knows
		(though anchors crossed as keys
may open it)
		that heaven does not move.

IV

I have been filling voids
		all of my life,
the void has now filled me.
When change becomes the rule
		of our daily bread
mouth breaks away from speech,
the intellect from mind
and mind, as sovereign, as difference,
sole rules the bodies of the heavens
		wrapped in their own cognizance.
Sleep, banished sleep
		moaning over a distant radio,
music filling the train—
		all the compartments,
all the corridors,
		conductors, passengers,
			the driver by himself
where fire was, in days gone by,
		now electricity the queen
one zero one, and zero one,
			and back to one,

moves us throughout the planets
up to our future (infinitely) home.

V

Country of badges,
("the uniform attracts the badge"),
country of longing to belong,
land of identified
            terrestrial statuses:
from what initial loss
did you acquire this passion?
            Lord of the city,
his duties well defined,
            the sun badge at his breast,
the stars on breasts around him—
            his path through all our days
(and the days of the mother-fathers
            back into furthest time
their calculus so depthless
            it has foregone all our conclusions)—
his badge the city's heart,
            its shield in honorable times
and in dishonorable,
            its mark on all our doors
with angels passing over.
            Out starless, loveless, speechless men!
                        men of no meaning,
of minds so uniform you make no progress
for you have lost all semblances of order,
            of sovereign *gravitas*
                        and bounded heraldry,
(Rest, rest perturbed spirits!)
The land is a pleasant childhood:
            I never knew my own.

VI

On stage, in a rival city,
accounted once again the capital,
      older by far than mine,
(though God knows how much older
           this mine appears)
      dream prince emerges
in sunlike garments
lighthearted blood in color
and his princess
      in scintillating white.
She is no royal girl by birth
      but thinks herself one
for the dream's purpose.
They dance—as youth had danced me
      once upon ever.
The capital had raised a pall—
doom-laden cloud over my rapture,
it is too complex, far too ramified
      in all its streets and stations,
I can do nothing with it.
      How long an age
since exclamation crossed my lips
      yet, in the flowering of dance—
the way he burns down to her purpose
and lifts it up behind a curtain
      of vacillating snows,
the way her eyes follow her arms
and touch her hands extended to the sky—
each time, each time, in simile
      of rapture there,
ah then, as if the years
      had lifted from my head
and freed the breath once more,
      a fervent sigh
      escapes me: I am born again
into an echo of enthusiasm.

VII

Cats scream in courtyards,
stench of their piss
cannot rasp clean a multitude of hands
        of their manifold murders.
Dream that became a nightmare
                hides underground:
Eurydice's kingdom
        I had looked for in vain.
Now she embraces Orpheus
        crowned with a wreath of thorns
inside a rose and tulip garland.
Stone frames on the subway walls:
pictures of people's happiness
        imaged over and over
                lacquer, fresco, mosaic . . .
in semblances still-born,
the gelid faces in archaic style,
        labor's arrested movements
toward the worker's paradise.
                Poets are searching,
clothed in their greatcoats,
        their plastic sacks in hand:
(the country's norm for every load)
        lyres in the plastic sacks,
seeking to lift the paradise-to-come
        back into open air
up the interminable stairways
        that men might recognize
their frosted future,
let it thaw out and come alive.
The silver swan of marriage
        winging from icebound river,
bright fields enameled by its flight,
        drives back the nightmare
down and away from where it tried to rise
        in the paralyzed kingdoms.
                Below the ground,
crowds are disgorging

every few minutes,
like lungs or bellows,
chest filling, emptying—
from out long marble walls
covered with ancient symbols
(corn, sickles, iron, hammers).
The dead have come alive,
long for imaginary programs,
futures no way prescribed—ambitions
looking to win the world back,
                    death into life.
Sparrows from this Atlantis
                    flutter still
          fitful above the waters,
from time to time they find a tree top
(the trees imprisoned
          in old palace courtyards).
          Mist-haunted winter's
crows, day-gray, night-black,
feast on the refuse of the giant river.

VIII

From glacial coast, in a waste of buildings,
so gray they are as carved from ice,
humans trod under foot by day and night:
          the dead coming up from the ground,
                    from the buried sun,
the live going down into the ground
                    to seed again,
along sky ladder, underground ladder,
                    met in one circle.
Meanwhile men drown at sea
          in frenzied combat hand to hand—
but conflict's in a tableau
          among a trove of pictures
deep in a hermitage
          of unnumbered monks
from all our royal quarters.

How shall we know then
the fate of one arrested man
          lost in this vintage?
The prodigal returns
forever to the bosom of the father,
the father's hand is stayed
by one of his three angels
          foretelling trinity:
cruel / kindloving / murderous.
Inside this it is possible to die
          suddenly in full flight,
among the great wings of desire,
the possibilities of anti-matter
beating themselves into the shadows.
          It is a thought that the last word
breathes out refulgent and is fully said,
or, much more often, only half said
                    as spirit breaks
on mind's huge ocean.
                    Three final songs
let there be sung in splendor gathering
                    a trinity of makers
          on living rock:
the man is visited by angels
their discourse inexhaustible,
          abyss of understanding.
But perhaps I am killing myself
inhaling the smoke of so many beings
in a world grown futile with fantasies
          divorced from all severity.
Time, I give myself time to hear angels
though it is hard for me to believe
          in anything beyond this dust.
Bring up a city to life
has been alive for generations,
tyranny-black, rebellion red
and it has turned to nought it seems,
          to senseless gold:
the salesman's ceaseless pitch,
a tide of liquid excrement.

The dead go down into the ground
                to the pulse of my heartbeat,
the living climb out of the ground—
I carry them—my breaking back.
                        Where will it finish?
Who speaks today of aims and ends
                when all have fallen into infancy
                        (though now I have not charity)—
the third man comes, nor young, nor old,
full grown into the garden of his love.
It is not possible to tell him from the angels
or to say which is which of the three angels
                        discoursing with the man,
who is himself all three.
Looks deep into the steppes around the city
(over vast glacial mounds,
                petrified dead of a late war,
over a blue cathedral shining in snow
sapphire and diamond emblem of eternity)
                        eyes level, rests his case.

IX

Have I arrived too late,
                        again too late
for all there is to know,
to do, to love and to forgive,
have I then come too late
                to end my life
with needful care, sterling intelligence?
Well, but allow the life to suffer
                if need be—not the word.
It would be better if the two of them
                could live unheeded
within some pastoral, post-revolution
                in a successful world.
In this however (romanticism if need be)
                there seems to have to be a choice.
It is my honor to choose the word alone.
                        Let that survive.

X

                      Time to begin again.
Thoughts of my city's labyrinths
          there at the midpoint—
the mind's adopted place—
        I rest once more in
                and will return to
time and again, I know it
       until the final transport leaves
       for a living furnace
burns to the end of all conception.
            City doors open wide
revealing experts.
       Wisest in all
the subjects of my youth, maturity and age,
      I make the calls,
the phones are working
and every citizen is of my college.
Or call out of the city—
everyone knows my books, titles and name.
The land is one vast dictionary
of nothing but the subjects I'm in love with.
          History ended,
knowledge expands in its parameters
as wide as my heart's university:
head has changed place with heart
          and heart with head.
Now it is possible to go into the streets
and smile not just at friends
but everyone in recognition.
The winds of sea-change.
         Landsmanship
parts me from all my previous countries
and gives me back my princedom.
Jewel of architecture,
           lodestone of engineers,
eden of planners
         of every stripe and color,
     race is abolished here,

all eyes are settled in their gaze
as lords upraise their crowns,
                    miter themselves.
          At last, a home, good God!
Names of the mother-fathers all recovered,
uncle from here, aunt from there,
most distant cousin from insignificant towns,
all now remembered through the smoke,
          and brought to life again
                    out of the ashes —
all reassembled, all transfigured,
                    a human reign.

ABOUT THE AUTHOR

For some forty years, Nathaniel Tarn, poet, translator, critic, and anthropologist, has been celebrated as an extraordinary figure in American writing, bringing to poetry an almost limitless range of interests and a remarkable dexterity in both open and closed forms. He has taught at the Universities of Chicago, London, Princeton, Pennsylvania, Rutgers, Colorado, New Mexico, and Jilin (People's Republic of China). One of the founding figures of Ethnopoetics, his work in a variety of literary and scholarly genres has ranged from Maya ritual to Jewish mysticism, the Buddhist monasteries of Burma, China, Tibet, and Japan to the Arctic seas of Alaska. Tarn has published some thirty-five books and translations and was founding editor of Cape Editions and the Cape Goliard Press in the sixties and seventies. His latest publications are *Views from the Weaving Mountain* (1991); *Scandals in the House of Birds* (1997); *The Architextures* (2000) and *The St. Petersburg Poems* (2001). Tarn lives northwest of Santa Fe, New Mexico.

Library of Congress Cataloging-in-Publication Data

Tarn, Nathaniel.
  [Poems. Selections]
    Selected poems : 1950–2000 / Nathaniel Tarn.
        p.   cm. — (Wesleyan poetry)
      ISBN 0–8195–6541–5 (alk. paper) — ISBN 0–8195–6542–3
  (pbk. : alk. paper)
      I. Title. II. Series.
  PS3570.A635 A6 2002
  811'.54—dc21   2002001701